This book belongs to

NICKI LIVINGSTON

…a woman after God's own heart.

Putting On a Gentle & Quiet Spirit

Elizabeth George

HARVEST HOUSE PUBLISHERS
Eugene, Oregon 97402

Cover by Terry Dugan Design, Minneapolis, Minnesota

PUTTING ON A GENTLE AND QUIET SPIRIT
Copyright © 2000 by Elizabeth George
Published by Harvest House Publishers
Eugene, Oregon 97402

ISBN 0-7369-0290-2

01 02 03 04 05 06 07 08 09 / BP / 10 9 8 7 6 5 4

Acknowledgments

How does an author ever properly and thoroughly thank a publisher for its unfailing support, unbroken encouragement, and unlimited vision? I don't know, but I do want to try. So "Thank you, dear Harvest House Publishers!" Thank you, Bob Hawkins, Jr., Carolyn McCready, LaRae Weikert, and Steve Miller. Thank you, Terry Glaspey, Betty Fletcher, and Barbara Sherrill. Thank you, Julie McKinney, Teresa Evenson, and John Constance, for getting the word out there! Thank you all for your patient assistance with my books. And now, thank you for putting wings on this Bible study series so that women can grow to know our Lord and Savior even better.

Contents

Foreword

For some time I have been looking for Bible studies that I could use each day that would increase my knowledge of God's Word. In my search, I found myself struggling between two extremes: Bible studies that required little time but also had little substance, or studies that were in-depth and demanded more time than I could give. I discovered that I wasn't alone—there were many other women like me who were busy yet desired to spend quality time studying God's Word.

That's why I became excited when Elizabeth George shared her desire to create a series of women's Bible studies that offered in-depth lessons that could be completed in just 15-20 minutes per day. When she completed the first study—on Philippians—I was eager to try it out. I had already studied Philippians many times, but this was the first time I had come to understand exactly how the whole book fit together and how it can truly be lived out in my life. Each lesson was simple but insightful—and was written especially to apply to me as a woman!

In the Woman After God's Own Heart™ Bible study series, Elizabeth takes you step by step through the Scriptures, sharing wisdom she has gleaned from more than 20 years as a women's Bible teacher. The lessons are rich and meaningful because they're rooted in God's Word and have been lived out in Elizabeth's life. Her thoughtful and personable guidance makes you feel as though you are studying right alongside her—as if she is personally mentoring you in the greatest aspiration you could ever pursue: to become a woman after God's own heart.

If you're looking for Bible studies that can help you grow stronger in your knowledge of God's Word even in the most demanding of schedules, I know you'll find this series to be a welcome companion in your daily walk with God.

—LaRae Weikert
Editorial Managing Director,
Harvest House Publishers

Before You Begin

*I*n my book *A Woman After God's Own Heart™*, I describe such a woman as one who ensures that God is first in her heart and the Ultimate Priority of her life. Then I share that one crucial way this desire can become reality is by nurturing a heart that abides in God's Word. To do so means that you and I must develop a root system anchored deep in God's Word.

Before you launch into this Bible study, take a moment to think about these aspects of a root system produced by the regular, faithful study of God's Word:

- *Roots are unseen*—You'll want to set aside time in solitude—"underground" if you will—to immerse yourself in God's Word and grow in Him.

- *Roots are for taking in*—Alone and with your Bible in hand, you'll want to take in and feed upon the truths of the Word of God and ensure your spiritual growth.

- *Roots are for storage*—As you form the habit of looking into God's Word, you'll find a vast, deep reservoir of divine hope and strength forming for the rough times.

- *Roots are for support*—Do you want to stand strong in the Lord? To stand firm against the pressures of life? The routine care of your roots through exposure to God's Word will cultivate you into a remarkable woman of endurance.[1]

I'm glad you've chosen this study out of my *Woman After God's Own Heart™ Bible Study Series*. My prayer for you is that the truths you find in God's Word through this study will further transform your life into the image of His dear Son and empower you to be the woman you seek to be: a woman after God's own heart.

In His love,

Elizabeth George

*L*esson 1

Counting on God's Grace and Peace

*C*ongratulations, dear friend. Because you have picked up and begun a Bible study entitled *Putting on a Gentle and Quiet Spirit,* you're certainly some kind of special woman! For when God lives within us, His Spirit causes you and me to yearn for these two precious qualities to be evident in our lives, as well as the many other godly qualities and behaviors the apostle Peter puts before us in the book of 1 Peter. For our purposes in this study, it will help us to know that...

As eighteenth-century theologian and teacher J. A. Bengel puts it,

> *Gentle* (or meek) has to do with the condition of the mind and the heart, and
> *Quiet* has to do with a tranquility arising from within, causing no disturbance to others.[2]

Gentle (or meek) means not creating disturbances.
Quiet means bearing with tranquility the disturbances
   caused by others.

Gentle (or meek) has to do with affections and feelings.
Quiet applies to words, countenance, and actions.[3]

But before we step into the meat of Peter's writings, it's good to note a few facts about the powerful book of 1 Peter. Many Bible teachers think Peter wrote these words around 65 A.D., around the time the persecution of Christians by Nero began. Christianity was beginning to be considered a separate religious entity apart from Judaism. Consequently, Christians no longer enjoyed protection from the government; on the contrary, they were coming under persecution from it. So prepare yourself to learn a lot about successfully handling suffering and trials and persecution, about holy conduct, about God's gentle and quiet spirit, and also about the amazing glory God promises to us afterward!

And now, to learn who this letter was written to and something about these special people, read on.

1 Peter 1:1-2

[1] Peter, an apostle of Jesus Christ, to the pilgrims of the Dispersion in Pontus, Galatia, Cappadocia, Asia, and Bithynia,

[2] elect according to the foreknowledge of God the Father, in sanctification of the Spirit, for obedience and sprinkling of the blood of Jesus Christ: Grace to you and peace be multiplied.

God's Input...

1. First of all, who is writing this letter, and how does he refer to himself (verse 1)?

   And what words does he use to address his readers (verse 1)?

   Note also where they lived (verse 1).

2. In verse 2, Peter uses yet another term to describe his readers. Jot it here.

3. Note the function of each of the members of the Godhead (verse 2):

   God the Father _____ us according to His _____

   The Spirit _____ us that we may _____

   Jesus Christ _____ us with His _____

4. How does Peter greet his readers (verse 2)?

5. What do you learn about God in these verses?

Here are a few thoughts that will help us as we begin studying this always-timely letter by Peter:

The Author: A fisherman by trade, Peter was called by Jesus to learn to fish for men instead of fish (Matthew 4:19). From that moment on, Simon Peter, or Peter, was one of the Lord's twelve disciples, along with his brother Andrew.

The Addressees: Most believe this letter was written to Jewish and Gentile Christians. The term "Dispersion" (verse 1) or *Diaspora* refers to these Christians, who lived outside Jerusalem in the five Roman provinces mentioned: Pontus, Galatia, Cappadocia, Asia, and Bithynia. Peter meant for his letter to be circulated among these brethren. These believers were also referred to as *pilgrims* or *sojourners*, which emphasizes their relationship with the world—they were strangers to it. And they were *elect*—literally "picked out" and "chosen," a privilege that began in God's original plan and purpose.

...And Your Heart's Answer

- Beloved, are you enduring any kind of persecution? Or are you suffering in any way? If so, how does Peter's prayerful greeting minister to you?

- And how do you think it ministered to Peter's persecuted friends?

- And how do you think the two virtues Peter mentions in verse 2 could equip them (and you!) to face persecution?

It's wonderful to think about God's grace and peace. They are two of the loveliest words God speaks to us, words that move our souls. But let's look a little deeper!

Grace is active and means "favor." So whatever your situation, whatever the occasion, you have God's favor. You have whatever it is going to take for you to endure, cope, have the victory, and be triumphant in it. And Peter prays that God's grace would be multiplied, in ever-increasing measure; that you will experience more and more of it, over and over again, time after time, in its fullest measure!

Peace, on the other hand, is passive and refers to rest. And so, dear one, whatever your situation, whatever the occasion or need, you have God's peace, God's rest *in* your suffering. Whatever the trial or test, *in* it you have not only God's power but God's rest.

From the Heart

We'll talk more later about what it means to have a "gentle and quiet spirit" and how to nurture this precious attitude. But for now, I want to share with you a common reaction women have when they contemplate a gentle and quiet spirit. Many times, the first words spoken are, "But I can't be like that! I can't remain calm when there's trouble!" True—if we're relying on our own strength.

But when we appropriate God's great enablers—His grace and His peace—we can achieve a gentle and quiet spirit. Thank God, who has graced us with these gifts, ensuring that we can do it. So, as we head into this study, let's try to remember three things with each lesson:

- We must count on God's grace. It's there. It's given. It's available.

- We must pray for God's grace. Just like a can of cola expands when we shake it, our awareness of God's grace expands when we "shake it up" through prayer.

- We must go right on with life...regardless of suffering. It's possible—and important—to have something positive to show for our suffering times.

Priscilla was a woman just like you and me, but she was an exile, a stranger, a foreigner, a pilgrim who was put out of her own country and sent away (Acts 18:2). Yet her pilgrim path led her straight into the path of the apostle Paul, to the establishment of a church in her home, and to an incredible ministry alongside her husband (Romans 16:4-5).

Jesus' disciple John, too, (the one whom Jesus loved—John 13:23) was sent into exile to the island of Patmos (Revelation 1:9). There, aged and alone, in essence a prisoner because he loved and followed Jesus, John experienced one of the most incredible worship experiences recorded in the Bible: He was granted a vision of God, which he then recorded in the book of Revelation.

Yes, my beautiful suffering friend, *as* we suffer for doing what's right and are enabled by the power of God's grace and enjoying His peace, *as* we put on God's gentle and quiet spirit and rely on the Lord instead of our human efforts and emotions, *as* we wait on Him to make sense and use of our suffering times, *then* indeed we have much to show in the end. Every time we endure hard times, we prove that the glory of the Lord is truly revealed in the end. As the psalmist declared, "Oh, taste and see that the LORD is good; Blessed is the man [or woman] who trusts in Him!" (Psalm 34:8).

Looking Forward to the End

1 Peter 1:3-9

*H*ow would you respond to an article or feature entitled, "Three Reasons Why You Can Stand Anything That Comes Your Way"? To me it sounds like a bestseller! That's the kind of information I would grab onto (and also grab for every friend of mine and every person I know who's suffering in any way)!

Well, dear friend, as we approach this next lesson, Peter has a powerful—and hopeful!—message for us as we suffer for doing what's right. He gives us three reasons why we can stand anything that comes our way.

Reason #1: We can stand anything because of what we are able to look forward to—the magnificent inheritance of life with God.

Reason #2: We can stand anything if we remember that every trial is, in fact, a test.

Reason #3: We can stand anything because, at the end of it, when Jesus Christ appears, we will receive from Him praise and glory and honor.

We learned in the previous lesson about our marvelous position in Christ and the marvelous grace and peace He extends to us in any and every circumstance. And now, Peter continues on with his letter of encouragement regarding the three reasons mentioned earlier that enable us to handle all of life. Read, reflect, and revel in the goodness of the Lord's provision!

1 Peter 1:3-9

3 Blessed be the God and Father of our Lord Jesus Christ, who according to His abundant mercy has begotten us again to a living hope through the resurrection of Jesus Christ from the dead,

4 to an inheritance incorruptible and undefiled and that does not fade away, reserved in heaven for you,

5 who are kept by the power of God through faith for salvation ready to be revealed in the last time.

6 In this you greatly rejoice, though now for a little while, if need be, you have been grieved by various trials,

7 that the genuineness of your faith, being much more precious than gold that perishes, though it is tested by fire, may be found to praise, honor, and glory at the revelation of Jesus Christ,

8 whom having not seen you love. Though now you do not see Him, yet believing, you rejoice

with joy inexpressible and full of glory,

⁹ receiving the end of your faith—the salvation of
your souls.

God's Input...

1. In Lesson 1, we learned that Peter's readers were strangers, pilgrims, and aliens. These dear strangers were also promised an inheritance in heaven (verse 4). Describe it here:

a._____   c._____

b._____   d._____

In the meantime, what was God doing for those saints on earth (verse 5)?

2. Moving on to verse 7, how does Peter describe the faith of the believer?

3. Next, Peter points out some facts about our relationship with Christ (verse 8):

I have not _____Him, yet I _____ Him.

I do not _____Him now, yet I _____ in Him.

Therefore, I _____ with _____ .

4. What do you learn about God in these verses?

...And Your Heart's Answer

- Note how Peter refers to suffering (verse 6). Share how his perspective should encourage us when we do what's right and go through trials. How will you put this truth to work in a current or future trial?

- Did you notice Peter's reference to the glory that the testing of your faith is sure to result in (verse 7)? It's exciting, isn't it? How should this perspective on the crucible of suffering encourage us when we go through trials of any sort? And how will you put this truth to work in a current or future trial?

From the Heart

We wish it weren't true, but suffering is a fact of life. It's just as Jesus declared it to be: "In the world you *will* have tribulation" (John 16:33, emphasis added). But aren't you glad that Jesus went on to add, "but be of good cheer, I have overcome the world"? Peter was present when His Lord uttered these precious insights, and Peter's words here in his epistle reflect the same truth. Yes, there is suffering, but we can experience great joy in our trials when, first of all, our suffering is for doing what is right, and second, when we look forward to the end and count on great glory afterwards.

In the personal notes written in the margin of the Bible of the great preacher D. L. Moody, these three thoughts about suffering and glory were found:

God has settled in heaven certain trials of our faith, which will as surely befall us as the crown of glory be given us at Christ's appearing. God's purposes of grace are a golden chain; not a link must be missing.

✱ When the devil tries our faith it is that he may crush it or diminish it; but when God tries our faith it is to establish and increase it. ✱

Persecution will be to us as the deluge to the ark—a flood to lift us toward heaven.[4]

—D. L. Moody

Dear one, we've been given all things that pertain to life and to living life in a godly manner (2 Peter 1:3). And that "all things" includes the grace to endure suffering for doing what is right. So when trials come our way, we can, by God's grace, put on God's gentle and quiet spirit, refusing to create disturbances and bearing with tranquility the disturbances caused by others. Oh, look to the Lord! And look to the glory He promises to His suffering children.

Questions I need to always ask myself...

✱ When someone is ~~wronging~~ has wronged me...
   ...do I dwell on it?
   ...do I complain to others about it?
   ...do I focus on it?
   ...do I react in the flesh or respond in the spirit?

esson 3

Gazing into the Mystery of Redemption

1 Peter 1:10-12

*I*n this lesson we contemplate the "mystery" of our salvation. As we'll soon see, our salvation was accomplished in a way that puzzled the prophets, the preachers of old, and the angels.

As we look at our salvation spoken of in these three sparkling verses, we will recognize that Christ accomplished the work of redemption through His sufferings, and that His sufferings have been revealed not only here, but throughout Scripture:

> We see in the Pentateuch
>   the Figures of the sufferings of Christ;
> We see in the Psalms
>   the Feelings of the suffering Christ;
> We see in the Prophets

24

the Forecasts of the sufferings of Christ;
We see in the Gospels
the Facts of the sufferings of Christ;
We see in the Epistles
the Fruits of the sufferings of Christ;
We see in the Book of Revelation
the Fulfilment of the sufferings of Christ,
and the Glory that should follow.[5]

1 Peter 1:10-12

[10] Of this salvation the prophets have inquired and searched diligently, who prophesied of the grace that would come to you,

[11] searching what, or what manner of time, the Spirit of Christ who was in them was indicating when He testified beforehand the sufferings of Christ and the glories that would follow.

[12] To them it was revealed that, not to themselves, but to us they were ministering the things which now have been reported to you through those who have preached the gospel to you by the Holy Spirit sent from heaven—things which angels desire to look into.

God's Input...

1. According to 1 Peter 1, verse 9, the outcome of our faith is the salvation of our souls. As we step into this passage, verse 10 continues to elaborate on that salvation and the interest that it has kindled down through time. How did the prophets show their interest (verse 10)?

And the angels (verse 12)?

2. What was the content of the prophets' message (verse 10)?

And what was the source of their information (verses 11-12)?

3. There has been (and will continue to be!) much about suffering and glory thus far in the book of 1 Peter. What additional information do we learn about each in this passage?

Suffering—

Glory—

4. What do you learn about God in these verses?

...And Your Heart's Answer

Do you give your salvation much thought, dear friend? I'm sure you'll think differently about it now that you know...

> The Old Testament prophets spoke about salvation without fully understanding it;
>
> The Holy Spirit moved them to speak of salvation by grace (and moved your heart to respond to it!);
>
> The New Testament preachers had the privilege of proclaiming it; and
>
> The angels (who cannot take part in it) are interested in the work of God in our lives.

The next time you come before God in prayer, thank Him for His marvelous gift of salvation. Then do as one saint of old explains: "The doctrine of man's salvation by Jesus Christ has been the study and admiration of the greatest and wisest of men. The nobleness of the subject and their own concern in it have engaged them, with most accurate attention and seriousness to search into it.... If it was necessary for an inspired prophet to [inquire and search diligently into salvation], much more for persons so weak and injudicious as we are."[6]

Jot down some "study plans" of your own for learning more about a few of the topics alluded to in this powerful passage of Scripture—topics like...

> —the suffering of Jesus Christ
> —the lives and sufferings of the prophets
> —the nature of angels
> —the role of the Holy Spirit in the life of a believer

Aren't you thankful for the Word of God? Study it for the rest of your life! What glory it will be to reach heaven and better see the unseen and better know the unknowable!

From the Heart

It's hard to understand all that's packed into these three treasured verses. But still we may respond in these ways:

Lessons from 1 Peter 1:1-12

1. Cherish the Christian's hope; earthly hopes are but castles in the air, delusive, unsubstantial; the living hope abideth.

2. Thank God for the hope of glory; it comes only from His mercy; it cheers us in our troubles, in the approach of death; in everything give thanks.

3. The heavenly inheritance is kept for God's elect; they are kept for it; let them rejoice evermore.

4. Their trials are precious; they issue in praise and honor and glory; let them rejoice even in sorrow.

5. The love of Christ gives the holiest joy; let us seek that joy in seeking to love Him more and more.

6. Prophets and angels love to gaze into the mysteries of our redemption; let us do the like.[7]

Responding Responsibly

1 Peter 1:13-16

*A*s our children were growing up, my husband and I often reminded them of the age-old principle, "With privilege comes responsibility" (see Luke 12:47-48). Well, my friend, that is exactly what Peter is now doing to the readers of his little letter of 1 Peter. He has just spent a dozen verses letting them—and us!—know of all the blessings we've been granted from the mind and heart of God. We not only enjoy the new birth and the living hope of a living Savior (1 Peter 1:3), but we also possess the glorious inheritance that is ours (verse 4) and the protection of God Himself (verses 5-12). What awesome privileges are ours as believers in Jesus Christ!

But, as the saying above goes, "With privilege comes responsibility!" *Therefore*...Peter writes, there are a few things you need to *do* in response to and because of these many blessings. What follows is a sort of "to-do" list from Peter for those of us who belong to the Lord and desire to make *His* characteristics the characteristics of our life.

1 Peter 1:13-16

[13] Therefore gird up the loins of your mind, be sober, and rest your hope fully upon the grace that is to be brought to you at the revelation of Jesus Christ;

[14] as obedient children, not conforming yourselves to the former lusts, as in your ignorance;

[15] but as He who called you is holy, you also be holy in all your conduct,

[16] because it is written, "Be holy, for I am holy."

God's Input...

1. Can you find the five commands given in the verses above?

   a.

   b.

   c.

   d.

   e.

2. What is Peter saying in verse 13 about your thought process? And where does Peter say your mental focus should be directed?

3. Regarding conduct, what does Peter say your consuming standard should be (verse 15)? And what area of life is dealt with in verses 15 and 16?

4. What do you learn about God in these verses?

...And Your Heart's Answer

- When Peter told his readers to "gird up the loins" of their minds, he was speaking to them in a day and age when both men and women wore long, flowing robes. In order to engage in any kind of strenuous activity, one had to gird up or tie up and tuck into a belt these hindering hems. It was their way of "rolling up their sleeves" for work, of getting serious about the business at hand. How do you think you could gird up the loins of your *mind?* And how do you think that would help you to live out your faith?

- Next, Peter advised those reading his letter (and that includes us!) to "be sober." Peter's call to sobriety encompassed moral and mental alertness. In others words, as Christians, you and I should not live our daily life in self-indulgence but in self-control and discipline. Ours should be a life marked by sobriety. How do you think you could better adhere to Peter's command? And how do you think that would help you to better live out your faith?

- Peter then moved to the issue of hope. His instruction is to "rest your hope fully" or set your hope fully on and in the Lord and His grace. As Christians, we are to set our minds on God's plans for us, to change our lifestyle to glorify Him, and to persevere during and through the trials and troubles that come to us. Well, dear one, with our hope set on the Lord, we can be confident. Is your mind strongly fixed and your hope set fully on Him? Are there any mental and/or spiritual adjustments you need to make?

- And finally—and most important—is the overarching theme of the book of 1 Peter. Peter calls upon the believers of his day—and for all time—to become holy like God rather than pursuing the lusts and wickedness that were previously a part of their lives: "Be holy, for I am holy." These were Peter's words of appeal, quoted directly from the Old Testament (Leviticus 11:44; 19:2; 20:7). At the root of the meaning of *holy* is being set apart to God in conduct and obedience. Therefore a Christian is one who lives the Christ-filled life. Can you think of any areas of your life where you need to be more obedient, where you need to be more holy in conduct?

From the Heart

Doesn't it stand to reason, dear one, that what's on the inside should and must come out? When God comes to live in us, shouldn't our lives change? And when we contemplate the price the Lord paid for our redemption, shouldn't it result in faithful obedience to Him? This is Peter's message to us. He's pointing out all that's given to us and happens to us on the inside when we're born again—the new birth, the inheritance, and the fact that we are kept for heaven and heaven is kept for us—which, in Peter's mind, surely(!) ought to make a radical difference in us.

It's true that as Christians we've been granted a position in Christ. But it's also equally true that our relationship with Him calls us to a certain conduct, to certain practices and efforts, to conformity to His likeness, to conscious behaviors...and changes of behaviors. And what does our Lord ask of us?

> To brace ourselves and mentally prepare for action, to run the long-distance race.
> To focus fully on living in a Christlike manner.
> To consider ourselves set apart *from* sin and its influence *unto* usefulness to God.

Oh, dear friend, we are called to God, chosen by God, saved by God, and declared holy as belonging to God; therefore, we must live for God. May we set our minds to work, "working out" His divine likeness in our lives day by day.

Lesson 5

Living in the Presence of God
1 Peter 1:17-21

What does your salvation mean to you, my friend? What difference does it make in your daily life to know that Jesus laid down His life and shed His precious blood...for you? Before we begin today's lesson, I want us to look at two saints who gave these facts some thought and then promptly made serious changes in their lives.

The first is Jenny Lind, a spectacular singer in the early 1800s who was known as "The Swedish Nightingale" and "the queen of song." When Miss Lind was asked why she abandoned the stage at the very height of her success, she replied, laying her finger on the Bible, "When every day it made me think less of this, what could I do?"

The second is a captain in the Army in the same era as Miss Lind, Hedley Vicars. The story is told that as he sat in a hotel room awaiting the arrival of another officer, he idly turned the pages of his Bible. His eye alighted on these words: "The blood of Jesus Christ His Son cleanseth us from all sin." Closing the Book, he vowed, "If this is true for me, henceforth I will live, by the grace of God, as a man who has been washed in the blood of Christ."

Beloved, the awesome facts of Jesus' death *for* us should make every difference *to* us! Today we learn about the high price paid to purchase our salvation—and the high price we should be willing to pay as a result. Read on...if you dare!

1 Peter 1:17-21

¹⁷ And if you call on the Father, who without partiality judges according to each one's work, conduct yourselves throughout the time of your sojourning here in fear;

¹⁸ knowing that you were not redeemed with corruptible things, like silver or gold, from your aimless conduct received by tradition from your fathers,

¹⁹ but with the precious blood of Christ, as of a lamb without blemish and without spot.

²⁰ He indeed was foreordained before the foundation of the world, but was manifest in these last times for you

²¹ who through Him believe in God, who raised Him from the dead and gave Him glory, so that your faith and hope are in God.

God's Input...

1. Peter begins this passage with a condition and a command (verse 17).

If _____

Then _____

2. How does Peter describe or refer to life as we know it here and now (verse 17)?

3. And note how Peter describes or explains our redemption (verses 18-19):

   You were not redeemed with _____

   But you were redeemed with _____

   And from what were we redeemed (verse 18)?

4. What do you learn about God in these verses?

...And Your Heart's Answer

• In the previous passage of Scripture, Peter called us to a *life of holiness*. His reasoning was that because of all God has secured for us, we should live as those who are called and set apart in and to holiness, as those who are "different." In this passage, he calls us to *a life of fear*. Peter's reasoning here is that a) because God is a judge (1 Peter 1:17) and b) because of the great cost of our salvation, that is, the precious blood of Christ (1 Peter 1:19), we should live life in utter reverence and awe and worship of God. This reverence, or fear, or reverential fear, is the attitude of mind in the person who is always aware that she is in the presence of God.

Dear one, Peter is calling us to change. He is calling us to live as those who once lived aimlessly, but now are redeemed by the precious blood of Christ. Can you think of changes you need to make in your lifestyle? And when will you put these changes into action?

* Now think about Jesus and the sacrifice He made for your salvation. Peter speaks of redemption as a technical term for money paid to buy back a prisoner of war. He also refers to the Old Testament practice of sacrificing a perfect lamb to atone for sin, a lamb that bore neither blemish nor spot. A price was paid for your salvation, my friend, and mine, too! We were not bought or redeemed with filthy money! Oh no! We were redeemed by the precious blood of God's perfect Son, Jesus Christ. How do you think a prisoner or a slave who was redeemed or whose freedom was purchased by another acted toward the one who paid the price for his emancipation? And how has Jesus' sacrifice for you impacted your life?

From the Heart

These verses speak straight to my own heart. They make me ask myself tough questions like, "Am I continuing to turn my back on my former life? Have I soberly acknowledged that God is a judge and will judge *all* people (including me!) according to their deeds? Do I live my life here in healthy reverential fear, not as one who's afraid of God, but as one who respects and reveres the All-Powerful One?" I know I never want to offend my God, or take Him for granted, or treat Him and His standards casually. I also know that I need to keep checking my attitudes and behaviors.

And so I ask the same of you, dear friend: Have you broken from the past? As one translation reads, have you broken "from your foolish way of life inherited from your parents"?[8] Have you taken on new behavior, the behavior of one redeemed with the precious blood of the spotless Jesus?

As we leave this solemn and wondrous truth, ponder these thoughts from another.

Suppose you are standing outside of a great auction room in London, and you hear a clerk say, "He paid $25 for a picture and another man paid $600,000 for one." You would instantly know quite a lot about the two pictures: The $25 picture may be any one of 10,000 little dogs done by amateur artists who paint sunsets, trees, and seascapes, hoping to get paid for them. The $600,000 picture—was it a Rembrandt, Michelangelo, or Raphael? You can judge the painting by the price that is paid for it.

We can judge ourselves by the price Christ paid for us, the depths into which He had to reach in order to save us. Christ died for our sins, and when I learn the price that was paid for our redemption, I form conclusions that are justified from other portions of the Scripture—how great was my sinfulness, the depths of my nature, and the height of His love.[9]

—Donald Grey Barnhouse

Peter, is forming these same conclusions about the depth of our sinfulness and the height of God's redeeming love. Let's be sure we live daily with these two facts in our minds...and an overwhelming love for Jesus in our hearts!

Loving One Another

1 Peter 1:22-25

*H*ow does your garden grow? Forgive me while I bring up gardening here, but it does have a place as we approach this next section of Peter's text—I promise! And, as I speak to groups on my book *A Woman's Walk with God— Growing in the Fruit of the Spirit,* I see many examples of decorating using the book's fruit-of-the-Spirit theme. Often a garden motif is used—some stages and platforms are miraculously transformed into gardens that rival the Garden of Eden, which was created by God Himself! As you know, the fruit of the Spirit (listed in Galatians 5:22-23) are nine qualities of life that the indwelling of God the Holy Spirit produces in our lives when we are abiding in Him and walking with Him by His Spirit. And what is the first quality that life in Christ should manifest in us? It's *love.* That's where Peter begins this lesson as he shares about the difference that God's salvation should make in our relationships with others. Join him as he explains:

39

1 *Peter* 1:22-25

²² Since you have purified your souls in obeying the truth through the Spirit in sincere love of the brethren, love one another fervently with a pure heart,

²³ having been born again, not of corruptible seed but incorruptible, through the word of God which lives and abides forever,

²⁴ because "All flesh is as grass, and all the glory of man as the flower of the grass. The grass withers, and its flower falls away,

²⁵ but the word of the LORD endures forever." Now this is the word which by the gospel was preached to you.

God's Input...

Peter has just finished a rather long passage about our salvation and the effect it should have on the way you and I live each day—in sober-mindedness, in obedience, in holiness, and in fear. Now he turns to the effect our salvation should have on our relationships with *others*.

1. Write out God's command in verse 22.

   What is the reason for this command (verse 22)?

2. Peter refers again to our salvation. How were we born again, or what was the active agent of our rebirth (verse 23)?

Describe that agent:

It is *not* _____.

But it *is* _____.

3. What happens to things that are "perishable," according to verse 24?

And what happens to the imperishable word of the Lord (verse 25)?

4. What do you learn about God in these verses?

...And Your Heart's Answer

• When it comes to our relationships with others, Peter clearly calls us to "love one another" (verse 22). But he also adds three words to describe the intensity of the love we are to have for others.

1. *Sincerely*—This means a love that does not pretend or merely "play-act." We are not to merely express love verbally and in gushy terms, but to genuinely love one another. As the apostle John wrote, "My little children, let us not love in word or in tongue, but in deed and in truth" (1 John 3:18). Sincere love holds no inward grudges while pretending love on the outside, has no ulterior motives, and wants nothing from the one loved. Now, dear friend, is there any person in your life who is not receiving your "sincere" love? What will you do to live out God's command to sincerely love that individual?

2. *Fervently*—In addition to our love for one another being sincere, it must also be fervent. In other words, we are to love with an intense love, a stretched-out-to-the-farthest-point love. Our love is to be limitless (to the limit) and withholding nothing (to the max). This is not a warm, fuzzy kind of love, but one that is literally "at full stretch," all-out, with gusto, if you will. So, when it comes to the general level of the fervency of your love toward others, on an intensity scale of 1 to 5 (5 being full intensity), how would you rate yourself? And what will you do to move your score up the scale? That's Peter's summons to you.

3. *Heartily*—Peter adds the quality of heartiness to the kind of love he calls us to. A hearty love comes *from* the heart and is lived out *with* the heart. It bids you and me to love one another "with *all* our heart," wholeheartedly and with all our strength. Yes, love is truly a matter of the heart. How is your heart measuring up? Any changes you plan to put into practice?

From the Heart

Well, my friend, it's easy to see that the kind of love God is calling us to exhibit—sincere, fervent, hearty love—will cost us greatly and will require much effort...and may cause us much suffering. And we'll have to put on God's gentle and quiet spirit to endure any ill treatment and still give love in return. Remember that a gentle spirit does not cause disturbances, and a quiet spirit does not react to the disturbances caused by others. Instead, we love—earnestly, genuinely, and whole-heartedly—even those who cause us to suffer. It's just as someone has observed: "Wherever you find love, you find self-denial."

This message from God regarding our "love life" is life-changing...and life-challenging! But we can obey it, dear one. The love that God has shown to you and me must now be shown by us to others. The love that God demonstrated toward us—while we were unlovely and vile sinners—we are to turn around and now demonstrate toward others, even those who are unlovely and vile sinners. It's easy to talk about how much we love God, but loving others reveals how much we truly love God. It's a supernatural display of God-in-us; and where love resides, God abides.

I want to leave you with something practical, a way to put feet on the love of God that is shed abroad in our hearts (Romans 5:5). These "love prompts" from an unknown person seem to be practical indeed!

True love is...
   ...slow to suspect,
    ...slow to condemn,
     ...slow to offend,
      ...slow to expose,
       ...slow to reprimand,
        ...slow to belittle,
         ...slow to demand,
          ...slow to provoke,
           ...slow to hinder,
            ...slow to resent.[10]

Lesson 7

Growing Up in Him

1 Peter 2:1-3

*H*ave you ever sung the popular version of the song drawn from Psalm 42:1: "As the deer pants for the water brooks, so pants my soul for You, O God"? How lovely the image of that deer so thirsty that it *pants* for water. Even more, how lovely the thought of a soul—our own soul!—panting for the Lord!

Well, dear one, in the lesson before us, Peter directs us to something we are to pant for and yearn for and long for. *As* a deer desires the water that sustains its life, and *as* the Psalmist longs for the salvation of the Lord (Psalm 119:174), you and I are to yearn for the Word of God *as* a baby yearns for milk (1 Peter 2:2). The same strong word is used for each of these three pictures and in each of these three scriptural references.

Beloved, Peter's point is clear: To study God's Word should never be a labor but a delight instead. Before we

look to Peter's message, consider these lovely lines of poetry
that lift up the Scriptures for us to admire...and long for:

> It is Truth sent down from heaven;
> > It is much to be desired;
> It is perfect, pure and cleansing;
> > It is every whit inspired.
> It is manna for the hungry;
> > It is milk to make us grow;
> It is light for every traveler;
> > It is Truth that all should know.
> > > —Anonymous

1 Peter 2:1-3

[1] Therefore, laying aside all malice, all guile,
hypocrisy, envy, and all evil speaking,

[2] as newborn babes, desire the pure milk of the
word, that you may grow thereby,

[3] if indeed you have tasted that the Lord is gracious.

God's Input...

1. Do you recall the subject of our previous lesson? It was
Peter's command to us to "love one another," to love our
brothers and sisters in Christ sincerely, fervently, and
heartily. In this current package of instruction, Peter gets
specific: He tells us how to do just that. First of all, Peter
exhorts us to discard some behaviors and attitudes. What
are they? (verse 1):

Discard or put away or lay aside...

a.

b.

c.

d.

e.

And what comprehensive word does Peter use several times in verse 1 to emphasize the extent of his command?

2. Next, Peter commends to us a positive action that will make it possible to love others, thereby displaying the essential behavior that God says characterizes believers.

Desire—What does Peter say we are to desire (verse 2)?

How does Peter describe the Word of God?

And how strongly should we desire it?

And how will the Word of God benefit us?

3. What does this passage of Scripture tell us about God (verse 3)?

...And Your Heart's Answer

• *Discard*—Peter points to five appalling attitudes and behaviors that have no place in a believer's life. What are your plans for discarding...

1. All malice? (*Malice* means desiring to harm others and doing evil.)

2. All guile? (*Guile* or *deceit* refers to deliberately tricking and/or misleading others by lying.)

3. Hypocrisy? (*Hypocrisy* is a term originally used of an actor, one who says one thing and does another.)

4. Envy? (*Envy* is a state of discontent and resentment that arises from desiring something possessed by someone else.)

5. All evil speaking? (*Evil speaking* wraps its arms around all slander, gossip, rumor-spreading, and verbalization of anything that would ruin the reputation of another.)

- *Desire*—One characteristic of children is a desire to grow up. As children of God, we, too, should desire to "grow up," to mature in Christlikeness. Peter tells us that the key way for us to grow is by desiring the pure milk of the Word of God just as a newborn baby desires milk. In my book *A Woman After God's Own Heart*™, I shared the following:

> There are three stages in Bible reading:
>
> 1. the cod-liver-oil stage when you take it like medicine;
> 2. the shredded-wheat stage when it's nourishing but dry; and
> 3. the peaches-and-cream stage when it's consumed with passion and pleasure.[11]

Which stage best describes your recent times in God's Word?

What steps could you take to reach "the peaches-and-cream stage" if you're not there now?

From the Heart

Beloved, it's never too late to "grow up." It's never too late to discard behaviors that are unlike our God. And it's never too late to embrace the spiritual truths found in God's Word. *Discarding* the bad and *desiring* the good should be actions we take each and every day of our life! Peter is writing to Christians, some of whom had been believers for as many as 30 years! His point is that believers should *always* crave the Word of God—indeed craving more and more of it. Oh, how I hope and pray that is true of me...and of you!

And so, dear one, we, too, are called to *discard* and to *desire*. When Peter tells us to lay aside evil thoughts and deeds, he means for us to strip them off like we strip off soiled clothes. That's the literal meaning of Peter's command. You know the scene: Your clothes are so dirty that you can hardly wait to peel them off and toss them into the dirty-clothes basket! That's how we must look at such awful behaviors as malice, guile, hypocrisy, envy, and evil speaking. They must be viewed as being as repulsive and as offensive as gross, filthy, grimy clothes.

I know that, in my past, I had a serious struggle with gossip. Even though I knew God spoke generally to all believers about gossip (here in 1 Peter) and specifically to women about not gossiping (1 Timothy 3:11 and Titus 2:3),

I did it anyway! But through constant and consistent prayer and through decisions made to eliminate certain patterns (and people!) from my life, I was finally able to "strip off" a great deal of gossip from my life. Sure, I've had lapses (more than I'd like to report!), but because of my personal desire to "grow up" and because of the instruction (and conviction) of God's Word, I've stripped off (and try to strip off each day) what was a habit of gossiping.

It's always good to take an inventory. Here, Peter gives us five practices that we're to peel off and put away. I know I'm taking my own inventory! Are there any attitudes or actions in Peter's list that you need to rid yourself of? Aren't you glad we can look to God for His gracious help?

Lesson 8

Building God's House

1 Peter 2:4-8

ave you ever had to do anything by yourself? Utterly alone? Have you ever been the *only one* bearing the full weight of a task or an endeavor on your own shoulders? And have you ever wished for someone—anyone!—to come alongside you and give a helping hand, to assist you in carrying just a part of your responsibility? Everyone knows it's hard to work alone and to stand alone. Being part of a group certainly has tremendous benefits!

And that's the way it is in the body of Christ, dear one. No one of us is ever alone. We will never be asked to stand alone or minister alone. Why? Because we are a "spiritual house" that is constructed and made up of many individual "living stones."

Hear the apostle Peter now as he writes to the believers who were scattered in the various provinces of Asia Minor.

Perhaps these dear folks were feeling like they were alone, the only ones "out there," having to bear their responsibilities and burdens alone. Peter reminds them that they are not!

1 Peter 2:4-8

⁴ Coming to Him as to a living stone, rejected indeed by men, but chosen by God and precious,

⁵ you also, as living stones, are being built up a spiritual house, a holy priesthood, to offer up spiritual sacrifices acceptable to God through Jesus Christ.

⁶ Therefore it is also contained in the Scripture, "Behold, I lay in Zion a chief cornerstone, elect, precious, And he who believes on Him will by no means be put to shame."

⁷ Therefore, to you who believe, He is precious; but to those who are disobedient, "The stone which the builders rejected Has become the chief cornerstone,"

⁸ and "A stone of stumbling and a rock of offense." They stumble, being disobedient to the word, to which they also were appointed.

God's Input...

1. First, Peter begins with Jesus. What metaphor or analogy does Peter use to describe Jesus (verse 4)?

   And how does Peter say Jesus is viewed by men (verse 4)?

And how is Jesus viewed by God (verse 4)?

Going on to use an Old Testament scripture (Isaiah 28:16), how does Peter further describe Jesus (verse 6)?

And how is Jesus viewed by those who believe in Him (verse 7)?

And by those who do not believe in Him (verse 8)?

2. What is the promise given to those of us who believe (verse 6)?

3. Peter also includes a metaphor or analogy for believers. What is it (verse 5)?

What is happening to believers (verse 5)?

How else does Peter refer to believers in Jesus Christ (verse 5)?

And what is their purpose (verse 5)?

4. What do these verses teach us about God?

...And Your Heart's Answer

• Just as a point of review, notice how the truths from our previous lesson tie into this lesson:

Salvation calls for loving one another (1 Peter 1:22),
which calls for putting away sins against one another
(1 Peter 2:1),
so that we can grow (1 Peter 2:2),
because we are a body, a spiritual house, a temple
(1 Peter 2:5),
and because this spiritual house is built with living
stones (1 Peter 2:5).

In a sentence, what is Peter teaching us about...

...our relationship to Christ?

...our relationship to other Christians?

- Why is it important for you to be a vital part of your church? What goal can you set for this week to put away sin, join in love, and "offer up a spiritual sacrifice" alongside those in your church?

- What does this passage teach you about God?

From the Heart

I thank God for Peter, the verbal artist, who has used superb imagery to paint a picture of the body of Christ that is simultaneously comforting and challenging.

How is it comforting? It ministers to you and me to know that we're not alone, and never will be. There's nothing we, as believers, will have to do alone or bear alone. Why?

Because we're "living stones," part of "a spiritual house," the church of God.

And what is this house like? Its foundation is Christ. As a house, it possesses strength, beauty, and a variety of parts; and is useful as a whole. What's more, this magnificent house of God is built up and improved with the addition of each and every new member that comes into the family of God (and that includes us!).

And how is the picture of the Church, the body of Christ, challenging? It requires that you and I as individuals do our part to sustain the strength, beauty, and usefulness of the house of God. We must also offer our own personal spiritual sacrifices to God. What would some of those spiritual sacrifices be?

> Our body (Romans 12:1)
> Our affections (Colossians 3:2)
> Our prayers (Revelation 8:3-4)
> Our praise (Hebrews 13:15)
> Our alms (Philippians 4:15-18)

May God be glorified and His house beautified as we offer up these spiritual sacrifices to Him.

Counting Your Blessings

1 Peter 2:9-10

Do you ever suffer from what many call "low self-image" or "low self-esteem"? Well, my dear sister in Christ, for a Christian these conditions simply need not exist! Why? Because of all that we have and are in Jesus Christ. Indeed, the entire book of 1 Peter thus far has offered an ongoing list of the benefits and privileges and assurances that we enjoy as believers in Christ. Peter has been pouring out his heart as he's been penning his letter to Christians down through the ages. He's been pointing to one advantage after another... after another...that are ours as saints. Can you recall some of them? Or, as the favorite hymn suggests, can you "Count Your Blessings"?

> We are elect (1 Peter 1:2).
> We are sanctified (1:2).

We have God's grace (1:2).
We have God's peace (1:2).
We are born again (1:3).
We have an inheritance in heaven (1:4).
We are kept by God unto salvation (1:5).
We are redeemed by Jesus' blood (1:18).
We are living stones in the house of God (2:5).

How's that for a list of blessings? And Peter has only just begun! And now, as we step into this next passage of the Word of the Lord, which endures forever, Peter's list goes on. Let's see what he adds to the list of blessings that are ours.

1 Peter 2:9-10

⁹ But you are a chosen generation, a royal priesthood, a holy nation, His own special people, that you may proclaim the praises of Him who called you out of darkness into His marvelous light;

¹⁰ who once were not a people but are now the people of God, who had not obtained mercy but now have obtained mercy.

God's Input...

1. In order to point out a contrast between believers and those who are unbelieving and disobedient (verse 8), Peter begins these verses with what word (verse 9)?

List the four descriptive phrases Peter uses regarding Christians (verse 9).

a.

b.

c.

d.

Why has God done all of this for His people (verse 9)?

2. We each have a past and a present condition. Complete this chart to more vividly see what Peter says about your life and mine (verses 9-10).

Past	**Present**
You were (verse 9)...	and into (verse 9)...
You were not (verse 10)...	but are now (verse 10)...
You had not (verse 10)...	but now have (verse 10)...

3. What truths about God do these verses teach us?

...And Your Heart's Answer

• Yes, Peter's list of our unique privileges in Christ continues! You are...

A chosen generation—You are an elect race, the people of God.

A royal priesthood—There is no separate priesthood in
   the church of Jesus Christ. Every believer is a priest.
A holy nation—You are a part of a distinct nation of
   people who are set apart unto God.
God's own special people—You are a people for
   God's own possession.

• Repeat again here exactly *why* God has done all of these
  wonderful things for us (verse 9).

God has done all this so that we may not only enjoy our
redemption but also proclaim the praises or the excel-
lencies and the virtues and the qualities of God Himself.
We are called to proclaim who God is and what He has
done—both by our conduct and by our words. How can
you do a better job of declaring the praises of God by
your conduct? And by your words?

From the Heart

So what's all the fuss about self-image? I hope by now
you can see that from God's perspective you already have
been blessed beyond measure! There should never be a
moment when we slump or fall into despair or discourage-
ment. There should never be a moment when we think
we're nothing or nobody! But, dear one, we do have to
remind ourselves to remember the many privileges we have
in Christ. And Peter has just added more wonders to that
initial list at the beginning of this lesson.

You are a chosen generation (verse 9).
You are a royal priesthood (verse 9).

You are a holy nation (verse 9).
You are God's own special people (verse 10).

All of this, my friend, was accomplished by Christ on our behalf. Some people base their concept of self-worth on their accomplishments. But, as Christians, we need to realize that who we are in Christ is far more important and meaningful than money, success, career, and educational degrees. We've been chosen by God to be His very own, and as a child of God—as one who has been purchased with the precious blood of Christ—we have worth that can never be tallied. Oh, thank Him now, and then refuse to succumb to feelings and thoughts of inferiority.

Lesson 10

Winning Through Winsomeness

1 Peter 2:11-12

gentle and quiet spirit. It's been a while since we've considered these two precious-in-God's-eyes attitudes, but in this lesson we begin to get to the crux of Peter's message—and to the condition of those to whom he was writing. Christians were being accused of defying Caesar, of causing upheaval and unrest with their new religion wherever they went, and of causing riots. But "pastor" Peter shows believers—both then and now—how to bear up under persecution. He gives us several for-all-times-and-for-all-circumstances pieces of advice to follow. And, my friend, we will have to don a gentle and quiet spirit in order to follow his advice and to endure mistreatment and misunderstanding. Read on...and then live on as you put still more of God's wisdom into practice.

1 *Peter* 2:11-12

¹¹ Beloved, I beg you as sojourners and pilgrims, abstain from fleshly lusts which war against the soul,

¹² having your conduct honorable among the Gentiles, that when they speak against you as evildoers, they may, by your good works which they observe, glorify God in the day of visitation.

God's Input...

1. Peter has been laboring to point out to his beloved readers (and us, too!) all that is theirs in Christ. And yet, as he's done before, Peter continues to remind these dear suffering saints of the responsibilities that such privilege brings. After all, Peter was present when the Lord said, "For everyone to whom much is given, from him much will be required" (Luke 12:48). Therefore Peter begins this next section of his letter with an exhortation. What is it that Peter asks his beloved readers to do as a result of their standing in Christ (verse 11)?

   And how strongly does he ask it (verse 11)?

   And why does he ask it (verse 11)?

2. Then faithful Peter gives a second admonition. What is it (verse 12)?

   What were the Gentiles (pagan unbelievers) doing (verse 12)?

And what does Peter say will prove them wrong (verse 12)?

...And Your Heart's Answer

Peter's words speak straight to our hearts regarding these issues:

- *The world*—Peter strongly urges us as Christians to remember our status in the world: We are sojourners, pilgrims, aliens, and strangers. As such, we need to remember that we live in a place that is not our home. We're simply visitors who are staying briefly in a foreign land. The world is not our real home. How do you view your life lived here on earth? What adjustments do you need to make in your perspective of the world or your ties to it?

- *The walk*—Nevertheless, while we are dwelling here in this strange land, there are things we must do and can do to keep ourselves from sin. Peter beseeches us to "abstain from fleshly lusts." That's the way we must walk through life here. You and I must abstain (meaning put away our sinful desires by controlling them right from the start). We must literally "continually keep away from" sinful desires. And that calls for us to walk with alertness and self-control. What adjustments do you need to make in your walk?

- *The why*—When it comes to why you and I must abstain from indulging our fleshly cravings, Peter supplies two reasons. *First,* so that our conduct as Christians honors

Christ. When we have our inner life under control, then our outer life will honor the Lord. And *second,* so that those who speak evil of us will be proven wrong. In a nutshell, the Christians of Peter's day were being falsely accused of every kind of evil imaginable (rebellion, terrorism, cannibalism, immorality, insurrection, etc.). For such misunderstandings, they were being ill-treated. Peter wanted them to make sure their lives were blameless so that those who accused them of evil would be convicted and might ultimately come to "glorify God," to believe in Him, too.

So, dear one, you and I must make sure our conduct gives no grounds for any rumors that may be spoken against us. As someone has quipped, "Is there enough evidence in your conduct to convict you of being a Christian?" In other words, does your good conduct negate any slanderous word that may be spoken against you? What adjustments do you need to make in your conduct?

From the Heart

Honorable conduct—now that's a wonderful lifetime goal for us! The Greek word for "honorable" is rich in meaning and implies the purest, highest, and noblest kind of goodness. It means "lovely," "winsome," "gracious," "noble," and "excellent." To live honorably means to live in a way that is so lovely that no charges against us can stand up. Attractive, gracious, upright behavior will always be our greatest defense...and our greatest witness. That's Peter's message to us: We're to live a good life filled with good deeds on a daily basis.

And a gentle and quiet spirit is a part of our honorable conduct. Mistreatment *will* come, but how you handle mistreatment will speak of your faith. Your honorable conduct, lived out in a holy lifestyle and with a gentle and quiet spirit, commends Christ to others around you.

So, do you have an unbelieving husband or children or parents or brothers and sisters? Do you work with non-Christians? Do you ever suffer for refusing to join in their antics or pranks or lies or immoral activities? Have you been called a "goody-goody" (which just happens to be the literal meaning of the Greek word for *kind*)? Are you continually misunderstood because you don't think or live like the rest of "the gang"? Then rejoice that you are wearing God's soft garment of a gentle and quiet spirit. Enshroud yourself with it, abstain from evil, and conduct yourself in an honorable and winsome way.

Respecting the Authority of Others

1 Peter 2:13-17

Oh dear! It's happening! Do you see the second word in the Bible text below? It's the word "submit." In recent years this tiny six-letter word has raised a ruckus around the world. But you know, beloved, this concept of submission to authority has been with us from the opening pages of the Bible. For example, in Genesis 16:9 (which was written about 1450 B.C.) God instructed Hagar to "submit" herself under the hand of Sarah, her mistress.

Well, today we begin a "series on submission," if you will. Perhaps it will amaze you to discover exactly how many people God tells us to submit to. For some reason, we have it in our minds that wives are the only ones God ever asks to submit. We are well familiar with the words "Wives, submit to your own husbands" (Ephesians 5:22). But we forget that Ephesians 5:22 is preceded by Ephesians 5:21, which tells all Christians to submit to one another.

Well, my precious sister, let's utter a prayer for an understanding heart, step into Peter's series on submission, and discover the many ways our salvation should affect our relationships with others.

1 Peter 2:13-17

¹³ Therefore submit yourselves to every ordinance of man for the Lord's sake, whether to the king as supreme,

¹⁴ or to governors, as to those who are sent by him for the punishment of evildoers and for the praise of those who do good.

¹⁵ For this is the will of God, that by doing good you may put to silence the ignorance of foolish men—

¹⁶ as free, yet not using your liberty as a cloak for vice, but as servants of God.

¹⁷ Honor all people. Love the brotherhood. Fear God. Honor the king.

God's Input...

1. Peter begins here where he left off in 1 Peter 2:12—with our conduct before men. What is his first word (literally one word!) of advice to all believers (verse 13)?

And to whom are we to submit?

a. verse 13—

b. verse 14—

And why (verse 13)?

2. What is the dual role of these two governmental offices (verse 14)?

3. What is the one thing we can be sure is God's will (verse 15)?

And what will doing good accomplish (verse 15)?

4. Note the four further commands at the end of Peter's instructions (verse 17).

   a.

   b.

   c.

   d.

5. What do these verses teach us about God?

...And Your Heart's Answer

Peter is passing on vital instruction here, my friend. He's telling Christians exactly how to live in a non-Christian world. And he starts right at the top: We are to submit ourselves to those in authority, which includes the ruling government.

But specifically what does his command to submit mean? Think through this list of definitions:

✓ The word "submit" means "to rank oneself under."

✓ It means "to accept the authority" of another.

✓ It is a call to "respect" the rank and God-ordained authority of another.

✓ It is a military term meaning "to arrange in military fashion under the commander."

✓ It means "to put oneself in an attitude of submission."

- Which ones of these definitions give you new insights into the meanings of the word "submit"?

- I don't know what your opinion is about today's government officials, but regardless of our opinions, what is God asking of us? And can you think of ways and areas in daily life where you can, do, and must submit to your country, state, and local leadership?

- There's a little "catchphrase" in verse 16. Did you "catch" it? Note it here and then share *why* we submit to our leaders.

- The Bible is all-encompassing. We, as Christians, called and set apart unto God, are sojourners and pilgrims passing through this world on our way to heaven. And yet we must maintain honorable social conduct as we live among others. Is there an area of social conduct noted in verse 17 that you need to consciously nurture? How will you do that?

From the Heart

I know it's always easier for me to do something when I know *why* I'm doing it. And it's true with submission. Here God tells you and me to "submit," but He also clearly tells us why. Did you notice these words in this passage?

> "...for the Lord's sake"
> "...for this is the will of God"
> "...as servants of God"

It's apparent that the *why* of our submission is all wrapped up in the *who* of our submission, God Himself. You see, *God* is asking (or telling!) us to submit; and *God* is asking us to submit for His sake; and *God* is explaining that submission is His will; and *God* is asking us to serve Him in our submission to others. As Dr. Charles Swindoll writes, "This recognition of existing authority, coupled with a willingness to set aside one's own personal desires, shows *a deep dependence upon God.* This submission to authority is not only *in respect to God, the foremost human authority*, but to lesser officials as well—kings and governors" (emphasis added).[12]

And here's another thought: *God is sovereign.* That means He knows all about the existing government and its officials, whom He has ordained and put in authority (Romans 13:1-7). But He also knows what He is accomplishing in His grand plan through these officials. As Psalm 75:7 reminds us, God "puts down one, and exalts another." And so, dear one, we simply trust the Lord...and submit. We never compromise the law of God as explicitly stated in Scripture, but on all other issues, we submit...as servants of God, knowing it is the will of God, and for the Lord's sake.

Lesson 12

Suffering for Doing Good

1 Peter 2:18-20

living faith touches every situation and acquaintance in life. Nothing and no relationship is left out. Peter knew that, and so did the Christians of his day, because so many of them (up to 60 percent!) lived in a form of slavery. While we don't face slavery today, for us to live out Christlikeness in every situation and acquaintance, we will need, once again, a gentle and quiet spirit. And so Peter and his readers have much to teach us about a gentleness that does not cause disturbances and a quietness of heart that does not respond to the disturbances caused by others. In this lesson we move from governmental authority to social authority—to masters and employers.

What have your work experiences been like, dear one? If you hold down a job now or if you've had one in the past, have you been blessed with kind employers? Or perhaps you've tasted the cup of cruelty? Of harsh treatment? It's our natural tendency to want to fight back against unfair and unreasonable treatment. But Peter shows us the better way—God's way—to endure ill treatment. Take note as Peter takes pen in hand and lays out God's plan for pressing on in a difficult situation.

1 Peter 2:18-20

¹⁸ Servants, be submissive to your masters with all fear, not only to the good and gentle, but also to the harsh.

¹⁹ For this is commendable, if because of conscience toward God one endures grief, suffering wrongfully.

²⁰ For what credit is it if, when you are beaten for your faults, you take it patiently? But when you do good and suffer for it, if you take it patiently, this is commendable before God.

God's Input...

1. *A note on slavery:* In Peter's day, slavery was a way of life, and many Christians worked for pagans as slaves or servants. Many in the early church who heard Peter's letter read were slaves, some to masters who were good and considerate, and others to those who were harsh and cruel. This was the situation of the day and the social structure of that time.

   The principles Peter lays down, however, apply to us today as well in employer-employee relationships. While we work for an individual or a company, we should obey the directives of our employer. And if we are asked to violate God's Word, we are free to change jobs.

On the heels of asking Christians to submit to government leaders and officials, Peter next turns to another area of daily life.

How does Peter ask us to act toward our masters/employers (verse 18)?

And what is our attitude to be (verse 18)?

And toward what kinds of people or employers are we to submit?

Not only to those who are _____ and _____

But also to those who are _____

2. Twice Peter tells us why we are to obey the command to submit.

Verse 19—

Verse 20—

He also points out two kinds of suffering (verse 20):

When you _____.

When you _____.

3. What do these verses teach us about God?

...And Your Heart's Answer

- We must remember that Peter is addressing our behavior
  as Christians (1 Peter 2:11-12). And beginning in verse
  13, he calls us to a life of submissiveness to authority,
  not only to the government and the "powers that be" but
  also to our employers, our earthly masters. What guideline does the apostle Paul give us in Acts 4:18-20
  regarding our submission to authority?

- Who are the "masters" in your life, dear one? Think of a
  few ways you could better submit, and commit yourself
  to them in prayer.

From the Heart

It's obvious from Peter's writings that there is...

>   ...a right way to respond to our masters—to submit
>   ...a right motive for submission—praise from God
>   ...a right attitude toward our masters—respect
>   ...a right reason for suffering—for doing good
>   ...a right manner for enduring suffering—patiently

Dear one, these "rights" automatically rule out a lot of
wrongs. The list is long: rebellion, anger, a bad attitude, hostility, ambition, disdain, discontent, pride, gossip, under-
mining, shirking, lip-service, revenge. I'm sure you could
add more to the list!

But here's a thought that helps us maintain our Christian perspective. It has to do with remembering...

Who's in Charge?

Because God is in control, we face each day with His power and love. If you receive some hard knocks today, turn them over to God. If you've been cheated, give the problem to God. If employees do not fulfill their responsibilities, admit your loss and trust God fully. Christians must never seek revenge, no matter how bad the circumstances. The impulse for revenge comes from people who think that systems or bosses or powerful people are in control. Christians believe that God has ultimate power.[13]

Lesson 13

Looking to the Savior

1 Peter 2:21-25

*W*hisper a prayer, my friend, for we are about to step on holy ground! Our Savior's suffering is about to be examined, and you can expect to experience both pain and wonder as you consider His sufferings. *He suffered wrongfully*—He did not sin; *He suffered patiently*—He did not react; *He suffered submissively*—He committed Himself to His Father; and *He suffered quietly*—"He held His peace." Behold the suffering Savior!

> The day when Jesus stood alone
> And felt the hearts of men like stone,
> And knew He came but to atone—
> That day "He held His peace."
>
> They witnessed falsely to His word,
> They bound Him with a cruel cord,

And mockingly proclaimed Him Lord;
"But Jesus held His peace."

They spat upon Him in the face,
They dragged Him on from place to place,
They heaped upon Him all disgrace;
"But Jesus held His peace."

My friend, have you for far much less,
With rage, which you called righteousness,
Resented slights with great distress?
Your Saviour "held His peace."[14]

In today's lesson, Peter tells us two things: First, some of the *facts* surrounding Jesus' suffering; and second, that we are to be *following* in His steps, just as a child follows a pattern in order to learn to write. Jesus is *The* Pattern, dear one! When we suffer insult and injustice and injury, we have only to look to Him and His suffering...and then to follow in His steps.

Let's look to The Pattern.

1 *Peter* 2:21-25

[21] For to this you were called, because Christ also suffered for us, leaving us an example, that you should follow His steps:

[22] "Who committed no sin, nor was guile found in His mouth,"

[23] who, when He was reviled, did not revile in return; when He suffered, He did not threaten, but committed Himself to Him who judges righteously;

[24] who Himself bore our sins in His own body on the tree, that we, having died to sins, might live

for righteousness—by whose stripes you were healed.

²⁵ For you were like sheep going astray, but have now returned to the Shepherd and Overseer of your souls.

God's Input...

1. In our previous lesson, we considered the fact that we and many other Christians endure grief and suffer wrongfully from the hands of others, specifically "masters" or employers. As we step into this powerful life-changing passage of Scripture, who do we find suffering (verse 21)?

   And what great statement and challenge is given to us in verse 21?

2. Peter tells us four things that Jesus did *not* do (verses 22-23). What are they?

   a.

   b.

   c.

   d.

   And what did Jesus do instead (verse 23)?

3. What did Christ's death on the cross enable you and me to do (verse 24)?

And what did He do for us (verse 24)?

4. What does this passage from the Bible teach us about God?

...And Your Heart's Answer

• We know that Jesus committed no sin. To follow in His steps, what known sins will you eliminate from your life?

We know that Jesus spoke no sin. What steps will you take to control your speech?

We know that Jesus did not answer back when He was insulted by others. What can you plan to do the next time you are insulted?

We know that Jesus did not react when He suffered. What can you plan to do if and when you, too, suffer?

• Is there a situation in your life where you need to commit and entrust yourself to God?

From the Heart

Beloved, this divine glimpse into the nature of Christ should and must affect our lives! These Scriptures are awesome! They are unfathomable! And, as I mentioned earlier in this lesson, they are certainly life-changing! These God-inspired words take us right to the heart of what it means to be a Christian.

Praise God that you and I have an example! We aren't asked by God to simply follow a few mere words on paper. No, God has given us an example to follow. We're asked by God to look to His own dear Son—His suffering Son—and to follow Him. We're to model our lives and behavior...after His! We're to pattern our daily living and conduct...after His! We're to do...as He did. And when we're unsure how to act or what to do or how to respond, whether in suffering or in everyday things, we can simply look to Jesus' actions and attitudes...and then do as He did.

Therefore, dear Lord...

May we ever seek to eliminate sinful behaviors!

May we speak only what is worthy of one of Your children.

May we render a blessing or bear quietly the insults from others.

May we suffer as Jesus did, as a lamb brought to the slaughter, for

He was oppressed and He was afflicted,
Yet He opened not His mouth;
He was led as a lamb to the slaughter,
And as a sheep before its shearers is silent,
So He opened not His mouth (Isaiah 53:7).

May we "hand over"—just as Jesus did—our suffering to You with perfect confidence in Your sovereignty and Your righteousness. Amen.

Amen!!

Lesson 14

Living a Lovely Life

1 Peter 3:1-7

Are you following Peter's progression, dear friend? Several lessons back, he began instructing us regarding submission. First, Peter declared that we are to submit to all governmental authority. Next, he advised us to submit to our "masters," our employers. Following that, Peter showed us Jesus as the ideal example of submission—the perfect Lamb of God who suffered wrongfully at the hands of harsh people. How sobering it is to see our sinless Savior submit... quietly and humbly...to such vile mistreatment!

But Peter goes on. And it's a good thing that we've just looked at Jesus, the Suffering Servant, because Peter's next words are difficult for some women. So read on, dear sister, with a prayer and with Jesus in mind.

1 *Peter 3:1-7*

¹ Likewise you wives, be submissive to your own husbands, that even if some do not obey the word, they, without a word, may be won by the conduct of their wives,

² when they observe your chaste conduct accompanied by fear.

³ Do not let your beauty be that outward adorning of arranging the hair, of wearing gold, or of putting on fine apparel;

⁴ but let it be the hidden person of the heart, with the incorruptible ornament of a gentle and quiet spirit, which is very precious in the sight of God.

⁵ For in this manner, in former times, the holy women who trusted in God also adorned themselves, being submissive to their own husbands,

⁶ as Sarah obeyed Abraham, calling him lord, whose daughters you are if you do good and are not afraid with any terror.

⁷ Likewise you husbands, dwell with them with understanding, giving honor to the wife, as to the weaker vessel, and as being heirs together of the grace of life, that your prayers may not be hindered.

God's Input...

1. First, note the four commands and their results that Peter gives us in these verses.

Two commands to wives:

a.   Command #1 (verse 1):_____

     Reason/result (verses 1-2):_____

b.   Command #2 (verses 3-4):_____

     Reason/result (verse 4):_____

Two commands to husbands:

c.   Command #1 (verse 7):_____

     Reason/result (verse 7):_____

d.   Command #2 (verse 7):_____

     Reason/result (verse 7):_____

2. What examples does Peter give to wives for submission and adornment?

a.   Verse 5—

     What key word describes these women?

b.   Verse 6—

     What did this dear woman do?

c.   Verse 6—

     What key quality describes these "daughters" of Sarah?

3. What does this portion of Scripture teach us about God?

...And Your Heart's Answer

• What difference(s) would practicing God's principle of submission make in a wife's relationship with her husband?

• If you are married, what specific change or changes could you immediately put into effect in this matter of submission to your husband?

And, by the way, how are you doing on the "without a word" instruction?

Just a note: Peter is not teaching that wives are never to speak or speak up. He is "speaking" to the issue of preaching and lecturing and harassing and goading and nagging and answering back. He wants our *life* to send a message from God to our husband!

Dr. Charles Swindoll adds to the list above. He writes that, even in the "silent" category, we are never to pout, sulk, scheme, bargain, coerce, or humiliate. He concludes with this thought: "Wives who use this strategy are not trusting God to change their husbands' lives. They're trusting in themselves."[15]

$\mathcal{D}$r. Swindoll writes further: "The tendency of many wives is to view their role in a conditional way that depends on the behavior of their husbands: 'I'll be the kind of wife I should be if he's the kind of husband *he* should be.' This passage, however, doesn't let the woman off the hook that easily. Peter has specifically included 'disobedient' husbands in verse 1, so he clearly has in mind women whose husbands aren't measuring up to God's standard.... Peter is saying something to these wives: 'You are responsible for *you*—not for your husband. That's God's job.' And wives who are truly obedient to Christ will find that he will honor their secure spirit.

"Yes, submission is a mark of security. It is not a spineless cringing, based on insecurity and fear. It is a voluntary unselfishness, a willing and cooperative spirit that seeks the highest good of her husband.... As he observes her compelling behavior—the silent eloquence of a lovely life—his heart will eventually soften toward spiritual things."[16]

- If you are single, evaluate God's call to a submissive lifestyle in relation to those people in your life. Do you have parents? Do you live at home with your parents? How could you begin to practice a submissive lifestyle at home?

From the Heart

Finally, we're at the heart of what it means to put on a gentle and quiet spirit! Peter has practically and systematically led us to this point: As citizens, we submit in a variety of circumstances; as slaves, we submit even to unfair masters; Christ submitted to unfair accusers; wives are to submit to unfair husbands. (And we're not done yet—1 Peter 3, verses 13-17 are yet to come, portraying our submission as Christians in an unfair society!). As a parting thought on this topic that is so vital to being a woman after God's own heart, consider these words by Bible scholar Dr. John MacArthur: "Here [in a gentle and quiet spirit] is beauty that never decays, as the outward body does. 'Gentle' is actually 'meek or humble' and 'quiet' describes the character of her action and reaction to her husband and life in general. Such is precious not only to her husband, but also to God."[17]

And now consider this prayer written by an unknown person. Perhaps it was written by a wife?

My Prayer

Teach me, Lord, to keep sweet and gentle in all the events of life, in disappointments, in thoughtlessness of others, in the insincerity of those I trusted, in the unfaithfulness of those on whom I relied.

Help me to put myself aside, to think of the happiness of others, to hide my little pains and heartaches, so that I may be the only one to suffer from them.

Teach me to profit by the suffering that comes to me. Help me to use it that it may mellow me, not harden or embitter me; that it may make me broad in my forgiveness; kindly, sympathetic, and helpful.[18]

Lesson 15

Trusting the Lord

1 Peter 3:8-12

*E*veryone loves (or should love!) an instruction book. It's a book or booklet that's packed full of diagrams, guidance, explanations, and step-by-step details that help us with some challenge or routine of our daily life.

Well, dear one, in this letter Peter delivers to his poor persecuted and scattered brothers and sisters in Christ an instruction book for suffering. He knew that if they weren't already feeling the harsh winds of oppression, they soon would be. (After all, as the apostle Paul had written elsewhere, "all who desire to live godly in Christ Jesus will suffer persecution"—2 Timothy 3:12.)

As you read Pastor Peter's "Directions for the Downtrodden," see if you can pick out his main points:

—There must be unity within.
—All difficulties should come from without.
—God will vindicate the righteous and punish their enemies.

1 Peter 3:8-12

⁸ Finally, all of you be of one mind, having compassion for one another; love as brothers, be tenderhearted, be courteous;

⁹ not returning evil for evil or reviling for reviling, but on the contrary blessing, knowing that you were called to this, that you may inherit a blessing.

¹⁰ For "He who would love life and see good days, let him refrain his tongue from evil, and his lips from speaking guile;

¹¹ "let him turn away from evil and do good; let him seek peace and pursue it.

¹² "For the eyes of the LORD are on the righteous, and his ears are open to their prayers; but the face of the LORD is against those who do evil."

God's Input...

1. Here in this passage Peter wraps up his instructions to his readers and to Christians for all time (and that includes us!) on how to live a godly life under persecution and in an unfair world. List the five social character qualities named in verse 8 that Christians need to practice toward other Christians as they endure ill treatment together.

    a.

    b.

    c.

d.

e.

2. In verse 9 Peter advises us on appropriate conduct toward those who are unfriendly and hostile toward Christians. He says:

We are *not* to _____.

   ...or to _____.

but we *are* to _____.

Why does Peter say we are to practice this behavior (verse 9)?

3. Quoting from the Old Testament (Psalm 34:12-16), Peter gives us further instructions:

   a.   Verse 10—

   b.   Verse 10—

   c.   Verse 11—

   d.   Verse 11—

   e.   Verse 11—

When Peter explains *why* Christians should exhibit such behavior, he refers to the Person and nature of God. Complete the following facts about God:

For the *eyes* of the Lord _____.

And His *ears* _____.

But the *face* of the Lord _____.

4. What do these verses teach us about God?

...And Your Heart's Answer

• It's been pointed out that five key elements are listed here that should characterize any group of believers:

1. Harmony—pursuing the same goals;

2. Sympathy—being responsive to other's needs;

3. Love—seeing one another as brothers and sisters;

4. Tender hearts—being affectionately sensitive; and

5. Humble minds—being willing to encourage one another and rejoice in each other's successes.[19]

Is there any particular one of these qualities that you need to pay closer attention to in your own life? And what will you do about it?

• And how is your behavior when it comes to those who are not Christians? How good are you at

—not returning evil for evil?

—not returning reviling for reviling, insult for insult?

—refraining your tongue from evil and your lips from speaking guile?

Do you have a plan in motion for success in these areas? What is that plan?

- How does it comfort you when you are enduring ill treatment from others to know that the eyes of the Lord are over you and His ears are open to your prayers, but His face is set against those who harm you?

And how does this knowledge about God help you to bear up under suffering with a gentle and quiet spirit?

From the Heart

It's one thing to deal with Christians in a harmonious, sympathetic, loving, tender, and gentle way (and Peter calls us to these behaviors), but it's another thing to bless those who curse you; to refrain your tongue from evil toward your tormentors; and to keep your tongue from sin when you are suffering at the hands of another. It's always easier to fight back and talk back than to bow the head, "turn the other cheek" (as Peter had heard Jesus say in Matthew 5:39), and "pray for those who persecute you" (Matthew 5:44). But, dear one, with the Lord at hand and with His soft garment of a gentle and quiet spirit about us, it is possible.

When it comes to mistreatment, you and I will have to choose whether to *react* or to *respond*. Rather than hate our enemies and retaliate against them and fear them, we must quietly—with a gentle and quiet spirit—trust in the Lord. He and He alone is in control of all things. And He and He alone knows His purposes in all things. And He *will* take care of His people...and their oppressors! With His eyes He sees all your misfortune and mistreatment. With His ears He knows your needs and hears your prayers. And He most certainly judges those who harm His people! Therefore, we do not retaliate. Oh no, we trust in the Lord instead and leave vengeance to Him. As He has declared, "Vengeance is Mine, I will repay" (Romans 12:19).

The assurance of God's care brings us much comfort along the way, doesn't it, beloved? It's just as an anonymous poet mused,

> Sweet thought! We have a Friend above,
> Our weary, faltering steps to guide,
> He follows with His eye of love
> The precious ones for whom He died.[20]

Lesson 16

Putting Christ First

1 Peter 3:13-17

I recently read a pithy saying that I think gives us the essence of Peter's message to us in this lesson. It reads, "Let your *lips* as well as your *life* speak for Christ."

As Peter writes to his suffering brethren who were living throughout the region of Asia Minor, he reasons with them. His thinking goes something like this: "Now, if you live your life in the way that a Christian should, in a way that is good and that benefits others, then you shouldn't have anything to worry about. No one should bother you if you live an exemplary *life*. But if you do the right thing and you're persecuted anyway, don't cave in. Just look to the Lord, stand firm in your faith, and make sure your *lips* speak well of your faith."

Yes, Peter has a practical "to-do" list for his friends and you and me on exactly how to live our *life* and use our *lips* in the face of suffering. Mark this passage well! You'll probably need its wisdom!

1 Peter 3:13-17

¹³ And who is he who will harm you if you become followers of what is good?

¹⁴ But even if you should suffer for righteousness' sake, you are blessed. "And do not be afraid of their threats, nor be troubled."

¹⁵ But sanctify the Lord God in your hearts, and always be ready to give a defense to everyone who asks you a reason for the hope that is in you, with meekness and fear;

¹⁶ having a good conscience, that when they defame you as evildoers, those who revile your good conduct in Christ may be ashamed.

¹⁷ For it is better, if it is the will of God, to suffer for doing good than for doing evil.

God's Input...

1. Peter begins this passage on suffering by stating a general principle in the form of a question. What is that principle (verse 13)?

2. Next, Peter tells us how to endure suffering for righteousness' sake. What should our inner attitude be (verse 14)?

And what should our response be toward those causing us to suffer (verses 14-15)?

Do not be _____.

And do not be _____.

But _____.

3. *What* else should we be prepared to do (verse 15)?

And *when* would we do this (verse 15)?

And *how* would we do this (verse 15)?

4. Peter's bottom line is that he does not want us

to suffer for _____.

but to suffer for _____.

5. What do we learn about God from these verses?

...*And Your Heart's Answer*

• According to this passage from God's Word, our goal
should be to live a life of goodness, to be blameless, to
live our life in a way that raises no questions nor brings
punishment our way. Are there any areas in your life that
need to be cleaned up and perfected?

- But, if and when you suffer for doing what is good, Peter gives you five aids for enduring:

1. *Do not fear intimidation.* This is to be your response toward those causing your unjust suffering. Oswald Chambers wrote: "It is the most natural thing in the world to be scared; and the clearest evidence that God's grace is at work in our hearts is when we do *not* get into panics.... When once fear is taken out, the world is humiliated at the feet of the humblest of saints. It can do nothing. It cannot touch the amazing supremacy that comes through the Divine imperialism of the saint's Lord and Master."[21]

2. *Do not be troubled.* This is also to be your response toward those causing your unjust suffering. Do not be disturbed in your heart or your thoughts. And do not join in any general panic, which can become a tidal wave. Instead, quiet your heart before God.

3. *Do sanctify Christ as Lord in your hearts.* In other words, put Christ first as Lord of your life...even when you stand before your enemies being threatened and accused. Those who sanctify and fear God in their hearts face challenges fearlessly. Those who do not fear God end up fearing everything.[22]

4. *Do be ready to make a defense.* Aldous Huxley, the famous agnostic, asked a man why he was a Christian. When the man replied, "But sir, you could demolish all my arguments in an instant. I'm not clever enough to argue with you." Huxley replied, "I won't argue with

you. Just simply tell me what Christ means to you."
We are called to give a logical, reasoned account of our
hope...without arrogance or belligerence.

5. *Do keep a good conscience.* Make sure your life
   matches up to your speech, and that you maintain conduct that is consistently good.

Now, dear friend, is there any current situation in your
life where you need to remember and apply these five
bits of instruction? Suffering can be caused by someone
in your own family, even someone right under your own
roof. Persecution can come at work from a colleague or
your boss. Neighbors, too, can be the authors of mistreatment. Plan to follow Peter's five pieces of advice and
pray to do so with a gentle and quiet spirit!

From the Heart

May I use this section to focus on Peter's advice to be
happy and to consider ourselves "blessed" when we suffer?
Perhaps you're wondering how joy and happiness can occur
in the midst of suffering and persecution. Well, consider this:
Suffering is the path our Savior Jesus has already walked;
and, as Peter told us before, "To this you were called,
because Christ also suffered for us, leaving us an example,
that you should follow His steps" (1 Peter 2:21). Also, as
we've already seen in our study, Jesus suffered unjustly for
doing good. When we're suffering, dear one, we must
always remember that our Jesus was a suffering Lord. And
therein we are blessed. We're allowed to taste the bitterness
of His sufferings...and the triumph of His grace.

Lesson 17

Understanding the Mysteries of God

1 Peter 3:18-22

A verse Bible scholars and teachers love when it comes to the unanswerable and un-understandable issues in the Bible is Deuteronomy 29:29: "The secret things belong to the Lord our God...." As you step into these next five verses from the Holy Bible, you'll find that most of it belongs in the unanswerable and un-understandable category and is catalogued under the subject of "The Secret Things of God."

But as we begin, there's no doubt about the boldness and straightforwardness of Peter's opening statement in verse 18: "For Christ also suffered once for sins, the just for the unjust...." No one can miss the point of Jesus' suffering and death on a cross. And that proved true of a group of African tribal people as a missionary was telling them about Jesus. In vivid language, the missionary told of...

the wonderful miracles and the sacrificial offering of Christ on the cross. Seated in the front row was the chief of the tribe who listened intently to all the missionary had to say. As the story came to its climax, and the chief heard how Christ was cruelly nailed to Calvary's tree, he could contain himself no longer, but jumped to his feet crying, "Stop! Take Him down from the cross; *I belong there, not Him!*" He had truly grasped the meaning of the Gospel, for he understood that he was a sinner, and that Christ was the sinless One.[23]

Yes, dear friend, Jesus took *our place* and died in *our stead. He* bore *our* sins, the just for the unjust. As you read on, ask yourself: Do I realize, as this passionate African chieftain did, that *I belonged there?* Have I received Jesus as my Savior?

1 Peter 3:18-22

[18] For Christ also suffered once for sins, the just for the unjust, that He might bring us to God, being put to death in the flesh but made alive by the Spirit,

[19] by whom also He went and preached to the spirits in prison,

[20] who formerly were disobedient, when once the longsuffering of God waited in the days of Noah, while the ark was being prepared, in which a few, that is, eight souls, were saved through water.

[21] There is also an antitype which now saves us, namely baptism (not the removal of the filth of

the flesh, but the answer of a good conscience toward God), through the resurrection of Jesus Christ,

²² who has gone into heaven and is at the right hand of God, angels and authorities and powers having been made subject to Him.

God's Input...

Hold onto your seat! You are entering a "heavy theology" zone! Many have considered these verses to be some of the most difficult in the New Testament. So to get ourselves started on a simple level, answer this set of questions meant to focus on the facts reported here by Peter.

1. For what reason did Jesus Christ die (verse 18)?

   What word is used for Christ's character (verse 18)?

   And what word is used for the character of those for whom He died (verse 18)?

   And what was accomplished by Jesus' death (verse 18)?

2. As you look at verse 19, what event is described?

   As you look at verse 20, what Old Testament event is referred to?

3. Moving on to verse 21, what subject is addressed?

And according to verse 22, where is Christ now?

4. What fact about God's character is mentioned in verse 20?

5. What does this portion of Scripture teach us about God?

...And Your Heart's Answer

• If you remember, the subject of the previous section of Scripture (1 Peter 3:13-17) was *suffering for doing what is right*. How does this passage (1 Peter 3:18-22) continue that thought?

• How could these verses regarding our Savior encourage you when you suffer unjustly?

The meaning of these verses is not completely clear, and scholars and commentators have explained them in many different ways. However, many learned scholars and commentators interpret them to mean that Christ went to Hades to proclaim His victory to the fallen angels imprisoned there since Noah's day (see 2 Peter 2:4).

From the Heart

Well, my friend, are you wondering what these inspired verses mean? You're not alone. I think the best way for us to take to heart these wondrous, mysterious scriptures whose meaning most certainly lies in the realm of God is to hear and heed the following advice.

First: When unjust suffering seems unbearable, remember the Cross.

Second: When the fear of death steals your peace, remember the Resurrection.[24]

Lesson 18

Making "the 180-Degree Turn"

1 Peter 4:1-6

*I*t's been sobering to read and study so much about Christ's suffering. And I've been trying to "get into" Peter's head to better understand his "heavy" message to his readers who were a group of scattered and outcast Christians who themselves were suffering.

We have to remember, dear reader, as we read Peter's heart-wrenching accounts and appeals, that he personally walked with Jesus throughout His three-year ministry on earth. He was one of Jesus' first disciples (John 1:40 and Matthew 4:18), preceded perhaps only by his brother Andrew. Peter had witnessed firsthand Jesus' anguish in the Garden of Gethsemane, His arrest, His mocking trials, and His mistreatment. And Peter was nearby when Jesus was nailed to the tree, and the cross was hoisted to an upright position. Yes, Peter saw it all and witnessed it all—the jeering crowd, the taunting thieves, the mocking soldiers, Jesus' cries from the cross, the literal agony and bloodshed of the Lamb of God.

"Therefore"...we can almost hear Peter wondering, "shouldn't Christ's suffering have some bearing on our daily lives? In the purity of our own lives?" And so Peter begins his next thoughts with a bold "Therefore"! His message is clear: Because of Christ's death for us, we simply *cannot* continue to live our lives in sin. Read on...and prepare yourself for change!

1 Peter 4:1-6

1 Therefore, since Christ suffered for us in the flesh, arm yourselves also with the same mind, for he who has suffered in the flesh has ceased from sin,

2 that he no longer should live the rest of his time in the flesh for the lusts of men, but for the will of God.

3 For we have spent enough of our past lifetime in doing the will of the Gentiles—when we walked in licentiousness, lusts, drunkenness, revelries, drinking parties, and abominable idolatries.

4 In regard to these, they think it strange that you do not run with them in the same flood of dissipation, speaking evil of you.

5 They will give an account to Him who is ready to judge the living and the dead.

6 For this reason the gospel was preached also to those who are dead, that they might be judged according to men in the flesh, but live according to God in the spirit.

God's Input...

1. What important fact about Christ does Peter restate in verse 1?

   And what strong command does Peter give as a result (verse 1)?

2. Peter explains that there are two ways of living life (verse 2). They are:

   a.

   b.

   What behaviors characterized our "past lifetime" (verse 3)?

   a.

      (You may want to look this word up in a dictionary!)

   b.

   c.

   d.

   e.

   f.

3. Peter warns us about what will probably happen when we renounce our old ways of life (verse 4).

Our former friends and acquaintances will

a.

b.

And what do these people have yet to face (verse 5)?

4. What do these verses teach us about God?

...*And Your Heart's Answer*

• The goal of the Christian's life is the freedom from sin, which comes at death. Therefore, as Christians, we should live the remainder of our life on earth pursuing the holy will of God rather than the lusts of the flesh (verse 2). How strongly are you pursuing the holy will of God in the power of the Spirit (Galatians 5:16)? Are there any fleshly practices and desires that you need to put away?

How does "arming" yourself with the thought that you can be triumphant in suffering help you in your quest for holy living?

• Have you experienced family members, friends, neighbors, or co-workers being offended or resentful because you wouldn't enter into ungodly pleasures? How does this passage of instruction help you to understand their response and your responsibility?

From the Heart

Peter began this passage detailing our obvious response to Christ's suffering on our behalf with the word "therefore," meaning "therefore" we should be seeking to live our life according to God's will and God's ways instead of in the lusts of the flesh.

It's true, dear sister, that you and I should be different from others. After all, when Christ lives within a person, His presence should make a tremendous difference, shouldn't it? As those who are "born again" (John 3:3) and are "a new creation" (2 Corinthians 5:17), change will occur. It will take time, but, as someone has called the act of becoming a Christian, it's "the 180-degree turn." The writer goes on to share his insights:

> Christians are an odd bunch. They don't plunge into every party. They go to church when other good people play sports, enjoy the sunshine, or catch up on sleep. They give money away when other fine people struggle along to maximize investment potential. They pray about matters that normal, reasonable, levelheaded people would gladly sue over. They poop out when the party heats up. They seem satisfied with monogamy. How quaint!
>
> A person whose life changes…at conversion may experience contempt from his or her old friends. He may be scorned not only because he

refuses to participate in certain activities, but also because his priorities have changed and he is now heading in the opposite direction. His very life incriminates their sinful activities.[25]

Can others tell that you're different, dear one? That you've made "the 180-degree turn"?

Lesson 19

Living in the Shadow of Eternity

1 Peter 4:7-11

*H*ave you ever stood in your church sort of dreamily singing along (and perhaps even swaying a little!) to the chorus of the hymn "Jesus is Coming Again"?

> Coming again, Coming again;
> Maybe morning, maybe noon,
> Maybe evening and maybe soon!
> Coming again, Coming again;
> O what a wonderful day it will be—
> Jesus is coming again![26]

All creation yearns and waits for that "wonderful day" when Jesus returns to right all wrongs and to heal the ravages of sin.

So how shall we then live "in the shadow of eternity"? How should the nearness of Jesus Christ's return affect our daily life? Peter gives us a few admonitions on how to prepare for the end times. See if you can spot them as you read.

1 Peter 4:7-11

⁷ But the end of all things is at hand; therefore be serious and watchful in your prayers.

⁸ And above all things have fervent love for one another, for "love will cover a multitude of sins."

⁹ Be hospitable to one another without grumbling.

¹⁰ As each one has received a gift, minister it to one another, as good stewards of the manifold grace of God.

¹¹ If anyone speaks, let him speak as the oracles of God. If anyone ministers, let him do it as with the ability which God supplies, that in all things God may be glorified through Jesus Christ, to whom belong the glory and the dominion forever and ever. Amen.

God's Input...

1. According to verse 7, how should we live daily life since the end of all things is at hand?

    a. Be _____.

    b. Be _____.

What admonition does verse 8 add?

And why?

2. Moving on to verse 9, Peter adds a command to _____.

And how are we to carry this out?

And finally (verse 10), we are to _____.

Why?

3. What two specific "gifts" does Peter point out in verse 11?

a. If anyone _____.

And how is this to be done?

b. If anyone _____.

And how is this to be done?

Why are we to do these things?

4. What do these verses teach us about God?

...And Your Heart's Answer

- Dear one, we are called by God to be "serious" or, in other words, not to be swept away by emotions or passions. This strong quality will enable us to maintain a proper eternal perspective on life. We are called to be "watchful" as in a watchful pursuit of holiness and the watchful attitude of a stranger, an alien, or a pilgrim passing through this life on our way to our real home in heaven. And prayer is the stabilizer, the constant reminder, the watch-guard of these two attitudes. How will you pray for a proper eternal perspective on life? And what difference should those prayers make in your daily life?

- Do you ever wonder what God's priorities for your life are? Well, right here in verse 8, God reminds us of Priority #1 in our relationships with others in the church: "Above all things, have fervent love for one another." A fervent love is a love that is stretched out and strained to the maximum. In the same way that a runner stretches and strains for the finish line, so you and I are to love one another. How do you think prayer will help you to put someone else's spiritual good ahead of your own desires—even when that person treats you unkindly, ungraciously, or with hostility?

- Yes, you and I are strangers in this world, but so are our brothers and sisters in Christ. So God next tells us to extend hospitality to one another, meaning "stranger love." We are to open our doors wide to one another and care for each other's needs while we are all on this earth. (Of course, this should be done with the blessing of your husband!) Can you think of ways you can extend hospitality to others?

- And finally God points to our spiritual gifts, those grace gifts given to every believer by which the Holy Spirit ministers to the body of Christ. These gifts are to be used in love and for the benefit of others in the church. Do you know your gift or gifts? You may want to prayerfully read Romans 12:3-8 and 1 Corinthians 12:4-10. Purpose to discover your gift, to develop your gift, and to *use* your gift! What does Peter say will happen as a result?

From the Heart

I don't know why, but this succinct passage has moved me in a fresh new way. It's so simple—and so simply stated. It leaves no doubt about who we are and what it is we're to focus on and do. I don't know about you, but this is exactly the kind of clear-cut instruction that my poor heart yearns for. I know that I've purposed a few things as a result of working my way through these few words from the Bible.

First, regarding self—I want to be more alert to my eternal perspective. This world is *not* my home! Therefore, I must battle the natural tendency to get too wrapped up in it. I must remember that the daily newspaper headlines are merely an indicator of how God is moving this world according to His plan. I must remember not to set my affection on the things of this earth, like possessions, property, and investment portfolios, but to set my affections on things above, where Christ sits at the right hand of God (Colossians 3:1-2). I must remember to hold all things lightly and nothing tightly. I must be ready—and willing—to move at any time.

And second, regarding others—I want to be more alert to my responsibilities to God's people. I need to live out love as a good steward of the manifold grace God has given to me. God means for my life and love to be centered on His people, not this world. His call to me is to love, to lodge, and to look out for my brothers and sisters in Christ. And I'm aware of (and impressed by!) the effort these three assignments from God take! Think about it: stretched-out and strained love, the work involved in hospitality, and the diligent effort involved in gift-development and use! I can only pray, "Lord, help me! Motivate me! Move me! Sustain me!"

But I know you join me in wanting your life to count for something, wanting your time spent here on earth to mean something (especially in the realm of eternity!), and wanting your life to bring glory to God. Thank you, Lord, for showing us *how!*

And now, O Father, we look to You for Your grace and Your strength! Amen.

Lesson 20

Growing Through Suffering

1 Peter 4:12-19

I wonder if you have noticed yet that a key word in Peter's epistle is "suffer"? In only 105 verses (the length of 1 Peter), the word *suffer* is used some 15 times, and here in chapter 4, Peter tells us how we *are* to suffer, and how we are *not* to suffer. I counted three times that *suffering* is referred to in just these few verses!

But, my friend and fellow pilgrim, there is an upside of suffering, as Peter shows us in these next sobering verses. It's like the man who was walking along a rugged, wave-beaten, ocean-sprayed stretch of beach when suddenly he came to a still, quiet area of sand. Why the change from a wet and noisy setting to this tranquil scene, he wondered? And then he noticed that far out to sea was a line of jutting rocks that served as a natural breaker to the wild surf. But he also noticed something else—an unpleasant stench! Yes, because of the breaker the water was calm, but it was also stagnant. Quickly he hurried along, much preferring the freshness created by violent waters and the scents brought by the wild sea breeze.

That's the way it is with suffering, dear one. It may seem undesirable, but it brings with it a purity and cleanliness, the blossom and growth of better things. Read on...and look for some of the benefits suffering brings to the life that seeks to glorify God.

1 Peter 4:12-19

¹² Beloved, do not think it strange concerning the fiery trial which is to try you, as though some strange thing happened to you;

¹³ but rejoice to the extent that you partake of Christ's sufferings, that when His glory is revealed, you may also be glad with exceeding joy.

¹⁴ If you are reproached for the name of Christ, blessed are you, for the Spirit of glory and of God rests upon you. On their part He is blasphemed, but on your part He is glorified.

¹⁵ But let none of you suffer as a murderer, a thief, an evildoer, or as a busybody in other people's matters.

¹⁶ Yet if anyone suffers as a Christian, let him not be ashamed, but let him glorify God in this matter.

¹⁷ For the time has come for judgment to begin at the house of God; and if it begins with us first, what will be the end of those who do not obey the gospel of God?

[18] Now "If the righteous one is scarcely saved, where will the ungodly and the sinner appear?"

[19] Therefore let those who suffer according to the will of God commit their souls to Him in doing good, as to a faithful Creator.

God's Input...

1. Peter guides us in the fine art of suffering. *When* suffering occurs, *how* does he say you and I should view it, according to verse 12?

   When suffering comes, *how* should we view it according to verse 13?

   When suffering comes, *how* should we view it according to verse 14?

   When suffering comes, *how* should we view it according to verse 16?

   When suffering comes, *how* should we view it according to verse 19?

2. Peter also cautions us. As Christians we are *not* to suffer for the following (verse 15):

   a.

   b.

   c.

   d.

...but instead we are to suffer for (verse 19).

3. Just a final thought from Peter: When judgment comes, where will it begin (verse 17)?

4. And, by the way, what does this passage teach us about God?

...*And Your Heart's Answer*

• As you look at Peter's list of evil acts (verse 15) for which we as Christians are never to suffer, how do you think being "a busybody in other people's matters" fits into this list? Are you guilty in this area? If so, what do you plan to do about it?

• On the downside of suffering: Have you yet accepted the truth that suffering *will* most definitely occur? Indeed, suffering is a given for the Christian. Rather than going into shock and thinking "some strange thing happened to you," how will you seek to welcome the reality of suffering in this life? What Scriptures from the whole of the Bible help you most?

• On the upside of suffering: Peter calls us to *rejoice,* to consider ourselves *blessed,* and to realize that when we suffer in the right way and for the right reasons, it *glorifies God.* How do these thoughts encourage you for your past, present, and future suffering?

From the Heart

In the book *Hope in Hurtful Times,* these words from C. S. Lewis are shared regarding the role of suffering and trials in our life. Lewis wrote of the trivia and "toys" that tend to occupy our lives...until some kind of pain comes along to topple our world and to turn our focus once again upward. He writes:

> At first I am overwhelmed, and all my little happinesses look like broken toys. Then, slowly and reluctantly, bit by bit, I try to bring myself into the frame of mind that I should be in at all times. I remind myself that all these toys were never intended to possess my heart, that my true good is in another world and my only real treasure is Christ. And perhaps, by God's grace, I succeed, and for a day or two become a creature consciously dependent on God and drawing its strength from the right sources. But the moment the threat is withdrawn, my whole nature leaps back to the toys.[27]

Beloved, thank God that you can be thankful for the suffering in your life! And beware of the trivia and "toys"!

Lesson 21

Joining "The Order of the Towel"

1 Peter 5:1-5

My husband Jim has been a part of the U.S. Army Reserves for 35 years. As his wife, I've witnessed 35 years of his rigorous training—both physical and mental. As a reserve soldier, Jim must attend drills once a month, pass a physical fitness exam four times a year, be tested on the battlefield and firing range annually, and participate in continuing education as a pharmacy officer. The Army's goal is to produce well-trained men and women who are physically fit, will respond to orders, and will work together to get any job done and every battle won. Each soldier is individually qualified for battle, and each soldier is trained to take orders from others.

The readers of Peter's epistle were experiencing opposition from the outside. The shadows of suffering were enveloping their ranks. Yet Peter knew that they must each

119

know—and fulfill—their duties and their position so that Christ's church could stand together in spiritual battle.

Listen as Peter (not a general, but a shepherd) instructs us.

1 Peter 5:1-5

¹ The elders who are among you I exhort, I who am a fellow elder and a witness of the sufferings of Christ, and also a partaker of the glory that will be revealed:

² Shepherd the flock of God which is among you, serving as overseers, not by constraint but willingly, not for dishonest gain but eagerly;

³ nor as being lords over those entrusted to you, but being examples to the flock;

⁴ and when the Chief Shepherd appears, you will receive the crown of glory that does not fade away.

⁵ Likewise you younger people, submit yourselves to your elders. Yes, all of you be submissive to one another, and be clothed with humility, for "God resists the proud, but gives grace to the humble."

God's Input...

1. How does Peter describe himself (verse 1)?

   a.

   b.

   c.

2. Name the first group Peter addresses in these verses (verse 1):

And what is his exhortation to them (verse 2)?

And how was this to be done (verses 2-3)?

a. Not _____ but _____.

b. Not _____ but _____.

c. Not _____ but _____.

And what will their reward be for faithfully carrying out these instructions (verse 4)?

3. Name the second group Peter addresses (verse 5):

And what is his exhortation to them?

And what reasons does he give for heeding these two words of advice?

a. Regarding the proud, God_____.

b. Regarding the humble, God_____.

4. What does this passage teach us about God?

...And Your Heart's Answer

- Three groups of people...and no one is omitted from Peter's instructions. Which group do you fall into, dear one? (Be careful! This *is* a trick question!)

- Once again, note Peter's advice to those in leadership. Even though you may not hold a position with a title like "elder" or "bishop" or "presbyter" in your church, you may serve on a committee or head up a group. How should and can you lead in the way and for the reasons Peter recommends?

- Look again at Peter's counsel to those he labels as "younger." How can you better follow his advice in this area?

- And finally, Peter gets to "all" of us with an admonition to be submissive to one another, and to be clothed with humility. How can you do a better job in these two important behaviors?

- How does the fact that God resists the proud but gives grace to the humble affect you? Can you think of any ways to minimize pride and develop humility?

From the Heart

Yes, Peter has a word of instruction for each of us:

Leaders are to keep on leading—even in the difficult times. They're not to quit or give up. They're to remain devoted and zealous and faithful. As missionary leader C. T. Studd reflected, "Sometimes I feel...that my cross is heavy beyond endurance.... My heart seems worn out and bruised beyond repair, and in my deep loneliness I often wish to be gone, but God knows best, and I want to do every ounce of work He wants me to do."[28] Men and women of this caliber keep on keeping on!

Younger saints are to willingly subject themselves to those who are in leadership.

All of us are to willingly subject ourselves to one another and to "clothe" ourselves with humility. The expression Peter uses here comes from a rare word which pictures a servant putting on an apron before serving those in the house. (Perhaps Peter was reflecting back to the scene of John 13:4-5, in the Upper Room, where Jesus took a towel and girded Himself, and began to wash the disciples' feet?) As Bible teacher and author Jill Briscoe has termed it, we're to join "The Order of the Towel."

So then, since we as Christians are to nurture a lowliness of mind and to gird on humility as we would gird on a garment, I leave you with these few practical pointers from my pastor: "To humble yourself takes 1) much prayer; 2) much rejection of praise; 3) much confession of sin; and 4) much confidence in a caring God."[29]

Lesson 22

Achieving Victory

1 Peter 5:6-9

As I previewed this lesson, I was thrilled to find three subjects that are of vital interest to any Christian who is endeavoring to live the victorious life made possible to us through Christ. Victory is ours when we understand our master, our enemy, and our brethren.

First, what kind of master do you have, dear one? He is mighty, and He is caring. You can count on Him. There is never a reason to cower or despair.

Second, what kind of enemy do you have? He is dangerous, and he is on the prowl. You must beware of him! Never let your guard down!

Third, and what about your brethren? They, too, are suffering in every corner of the globe. You must pray for them. You are never alone in your suffering.

What comfort and encouragement you and I can draw from this information, my friend! As we face our foes and as we endure mistreatment and misunderstanding, we can *look* to God, *look out* for the devil, and *look outside* ourselves in concern for our suffering brothers and sisters.

And now, from the pen of Peter...

1 Peter 5:6-9

⁶ Therefore humble yourselves under the mighty hand of God, that He may exalt you in due time,

⁷ casting all your care upon Him, for He cares for you.

⁸ Be sober, be vigilant; because your adversary the devil walks about like a roaring lion, seeking whom he may devour.

⁹ Resist him, steadfast in the faith, knowing that the same sufferings are experienced by your brotherhood in the world.

God's Input...

1. Good communication and good newspaper reporting always includes answers to the questions *who, what, where, when, why,* and *how.* As we'll see in this passage, Peter writes to us using these time-honored principles. Fill in the information yourself as you read the Bible text.

Who is described in verse 6?

What command is given to us in regard to Him?

Why?

And when will this occur?

What else are we to do (verse 7)?

And how much?

And, again, why?

2. Continuing on with our reporting and observation skills...

Who is described in verse 8?

What two commands are given to us in regard to him?

a.

b.

In a word, how does Peter describe him (verse 8)?

What illustration does Peter use (verse 8)?

And what is he actively doing (verse 8)?

What action does Peter advise that we take (verse 9)?

And what solace does Peter provide?

3. What does this portion of Scripture teach us about God?

...And Your Heart's Answer

• Just as a matter of review, it will help you and me to remember the flow of Peter's text:

✔ Verses 1-4 instructs *leaders* regarding their actions during suffering times: They are to continue leading.

✔ Verse 5 instructs those who are *younger* and, indeed, *all* of us, regarding our roles during suffering times: We are to submit to our leaders and be subject to one another.

✔ Verses 1-5 paint a picture of the singular attitude we are to have toward *other Christians* during suffering times. It is an attitude of humble submission.

✔ Verses 6-7 paint a picture of our attitude toward *God* during suffering times. Once again, it is an attitude of humble submission.

✔ Verses 8-9 paint a picture of our attitude toward *the devil* during suffering times. It is an attitude of deliberate resistance!

• As you think about your life—and perhaps your own personal suffering—how does the promise regarding God in verse 7 help you face your difficulties?

• And as you think about your life—and perhaps your own personal struggles—how do the facts about the devil in verse 8 motivate you to "be sober" and "be vigilant"?

How do you plan to "resist" the devil and stand "steadfast in the faith"?

Dear one, we are never alone in our suffering. And we are never the only ones who suffer. As Peter reminds us, every brother and sister in Christ around the globe experiences "the same sufferings" as you and I do. How can you expand your prayer life to include other suffering saints?

From the Heart

In our previous lesson, I shared about my husband's involvement in the U.S. Army Reserves. We noted that no army ever gets a job done without the cooperation, obedience, and response of its soldiers. In this lesson, we looked at yet another principle of victory—that no army ever wins a battle without understanding the enemy.

Beloved, whether we like it or not, Christians have always been compared to soldiers, and the battle that we wage against sin and evil has been likened to war. To adequately wage the war into which God calls us we need God's help, and we need motivation, training, discipline, and endurance. Victory also demands that we be both unified and aggressive. Unity is achieved as we submit to one another, and aggression is expressed as we resist the devil and the forces of evil. For you and me to carry out our responsibility as warriors, we must be aggressive in advancing Christ's cause both individually (resisting the devil) and with other members of the body of Christ (submitting to one another).

Are you actively submitting yourself to those in authority?

And are you actively resisting your enemy and adversary, the devil?

These two actions, dear one, stem from attitudes of the heart—and get the job done both in the body of Christ and against the outside force of Satan. As the popular hymn "Onward, Christian Soldiers" reminds us,

> At the sign of triumph
> Satan's host doth flee;
> On then, Christian soldiers,
> On to victory![30]

Lesson 23

Fanning the Flame of Faith

1 Peter 5:10-11

"Out of suffering have emerged the strongest souls; the most massive characters are seared with scars."[31] A strong soul and massive character—what Christian doesn't yearn for (indeed, pray for!) such traits? Yet these noble qualities, dear one, are often the fruits of suffering. Suffering hurts. Pain is unpleasant. Persecution is undesirable. And still we know that tremendously positive effects are forged in the fire and flame of suffering.

As you read and study this next sobering lesson on suffering, and as Peter lays out the positive effects of suffering, keep in mind that you and I can carry away "a souvenir," some positive blessing from our suffering. So why not choose to grow in faith when you face suffering head-on? As Adoniram Judson, the great early missionary to Burma, wrote to another, "I can assure you that months and months of heartrending anguish are before you, whether you will or not. Yet take the bitter cup with both hands, and sit down to your repast. You will soon learn a secret, that there is sweetness at the bottom."[32]

Let's look to the Lord and His positive message to us through Peter regarding the many beneficial effects of suffering. By the time you finish, I think you'll agree that suffering most definitely fans the flame of faith!

1 Peter 5:10-11

[10] But may the God of all grace, who called us to His eternal glory by Christ Jesus, after you have suffered a while, perfect, establish, strengthen, and settle you.

[11] To Him be the glory and the dominion forever and ever. Amen.

God's Input...

1. Here, my friend, is a passage that concerns life (when?) _____ you have suffered (verse 10).

   Peter repeats God's perspective again (see 1 Peter 1:6 for the first mention of this) on the duration of our suffering. How long will it last (verse 10)?

2. How does Peter refer to God (verse 10)?

   And what has God done for you (verse 10)?

3. If you have access to a dictionary, look up each of the following *verbs* from verse 10 and give a short definition in your own words. (If no dictionary is available, write out your own brief definition of what you think these familiar words mean.)

Perfect—

Establish—

Strengthen—

Settle—

4. Peter ends these verses with an acknowledgment of God as a constant source of courage and confidence (verse 11):

To Him be _____.

5. What does this passage teach us about God?

...And Your Heart's Answer

• After five chapters of instructions to Christians who were suffering, and after advising them at length regarding their suffering, how does Peter wrap up his letter in these two power-packed verses? What is the mood? What is his message?

- Earlier in this lesson we considered "the positive effects of suffering." As we prepare to leave Peter's treatise on suffering, consider these priceless positive effects of suffering:

  ✓ We will make it through our suffering. Peter uses the tiny word *after*.

  ✓ Our suffering is brief, only for *a while*.

  ✓ The *God of all grace* will enable us through our suffering.

  ✓ Suffering will *perfect* us. This is a medical term meaning "to set a fracture, to mend, to make right, to restore." Our suffering will complete us and mature us and make us great women of faith. I have on my library shelf a book entitled *The Hidden Price of Greatness*.[33] And it's true, dear one, that when it comes to spiritual maturity, the hidden price of greatness *is* suffering! As it's been said, "God prepares great men [and women!] for great tasks by great trials."[34]

  ✓ Suffering will *establish* us. This means to make us steadfast and as solid as granite! As William Barclay explains, suffering can have two effects on a person:

*S*uffering of body and sorrow of heart do one of two things to a man. They either make him collapse or they leave him with a solidity of character which he could never have gained anywhere else. If he meets them with continuing trust in Christ, he emerges like toughened steel that has been tempered in the fire.[35]

✓ Suffering will *strengthen* us. Do you want to be infused with power, my friend? Well, that's what this positive effect of suffering means. It is suffering that conditions you and equips you for active service to Christ and fills you with strength enough to go on. We can't help but enjoy the exquisite words of William Barclay once again as he explains: "The wind will extinguish a weak flame; but it will fan a strong flame into a still greater blaze."[36]

✓ Suffering will *settle* us. Beloved, are you fixed on a foundation? That's what suffering will accomplish in your faith. For, as Barclay again expounds, "When we have to meet sorrow and suffering we are driven down to the very bedrock of faith. It is then that we discover what are the things which cannot be shaken. It is in time of trial that we discover the great truths on which real life is founded."[37]

How do you think the truths in these two verses ministered to the original readers?

How do they minister to you as you think about any suffering you are enduring (or will endure)?

From the Heart

Oh, the grace of God! As one has said, "Grace is infinite love expressing itself in infinite goodness!"[38] Here, in just 41 words, we learn a thimbleful of truth about the infinite ocean of our God's grace. He is the God *of* all grace, who *by* His grace has called us to His eternal glory by Christ Jesus, who *in* His grace perfects, establishes, strengthens, and settles us. And, fellow sufferer, His grace is *always* sufficient, *always* all that we need, *always* there when we need it, and *always* all that we need it to be!

"The God of all grace." This exceedingly beautiful title applies to our Father in heaven, dear one. He has...

—Justifying grace for all believers,

—Illuminating grace for every seeker,

—Comforting grace for the bereaved,

—Strengthening grace for the weak,

—Sanctifying grace for the unholy,

—Living grace for the pilgrim, and

—Dying grace for the end of the journey.[39]

Bring your needs to the Lord, beloved, and discover the grace of God that truly and perfectly extends itself to each and every sorrow and trial.

Lesson 24

Living in Peace

1 Peter 5:12-14

s a writer, I know that endings are most difficult to write! Ending each chapter is a challenge, but ending each book is the hardest writing I do! Why? Because I want to end strongly—yet with encouragement to my readers. I want to wrap up a body of information—yet keep it short. I want to wrap my arms around the primary focus of the book—yet state it succinctly, directly, and to the point. I want to leave my readers with some kind of sensation—about their life, about their future, about the message, and about our God— yet motivate them to move out on the truths they've just learned. Yes, ending a book can take weeks of work!

Well, dear one, Peter faced this same dilemma as he was forced to lay down his pen. It's probable that Peter had not met those who would read his letter...and that he would never meet them! But knowing of their struggles, and being a shepherd at heart (1 Peter 5:2), Peter wrote. He couldn't personally deliver the strong encouragement they needed, but he could write to them. Yes, it was probably with pain and a prayer that Peter ceased his outpouring.

And his subject matter—suffering for doing what is right—was certainly something he knew all too well himself! You see, he had witnessed—up close and personal—the suffering of his friend and Savior. His was a front-row seat, if you will! Yes, he knew all about the cross, the hounding crowds, the belligerent rulers, the ranks of armed soldiers, the brutal trials...and the cross. God had certainly chosen the perfect person to minister to others who were suffering for doing what is right! And now he must close. Take note, my friend, of exactly how he does it.

1 Peter 5:12-14

12 By Silvanus, our faithful brother as I consider him, I have written to you briefly, exhorting and testifying that this is the true grace of God in which you stand.

13 She who is in Babylon, elect together with you, greets you; and so does Mark my son.

14 Greet one another with a kiss of love. Peace to you all who are in Christ Jesus. Amen.

God's Input...

1. Peter is signing off. He's wrapping up his letter. And in so doing he names names.

Who helped Peter write this epistle (verse 12)?

And how does Peter refer to him (verse 12)?

> Just a word of information here. Silvanus, or Silas, was a proven and faithful servant of the church and the apostles. His track record was long and flawless. Silvanus was chosen to deliver the letter from the Jerusalem council to the church in Antioch (Acts 15:11); had accompanied Paul on his second missionary journey (Acts 15:40–18:11); had helped Paul write his letters to the Thessalonians; and had ministered with Timothy in Corinth (2 Corinthians 1:19). He is definitely someone we can emulate!

What phrase describes the second "person" (verse 13)?

And what other person is named (verse 13)?

And how does Peter refer to him (verse 13)?

> And yet another note: This young man, who never heard nor followed Jesus, eventually wrote his own gospel account, which has been considered by many scholars to be "Peter's account." He had only heard Peter speak of the Savior and the details surrounding His life, which he turned around and shared with us.

2. What dual role did Peter have in mind for his letter (verse 12)?

What is Peter's final word of advice to his friends—and us (verse 12)?

What is the tone of Peter's closing (verse 14)?

3. What do these verses teach us about God?

...And Your Heart's Answer

• In just a few words, what does this passage from Peter accomplish?

• Do you think you can cope with life a little better, dear one, after making your way through Peter's passionate letter about suffering? How can you consciously re-member Peter's exhortation to "stand" firm even in the midst of suffering?

From the Heart

Beloved, Peter's final word to us is about peace. While writing my book *A Woman's Walk with God—Growing in the Fruit of the Spirit,*[40] I learned that there are two kinds of peace needed in the arena of life, both available to us from and through God—*personal peace* and *interpersonal peace.* I know you can relate to the need for interpersonal peace. Everyone has been in situations where there is strife and malice! And many times our suffering comes from the hands of others (which calls for interpersonal peace) and can tempt us to succumb ourselves to the level of strife and fighting (which calls for interpersonal peace). Thank God His peace—interpersonal peace—is available from His Holy Spirit. And so Peter ends, "Peace to you all who are in Christ Jesus."

And then there is the area of *personal peace,* which is sorely needed when facing terror, fear, panic, dread, doubt, and restlessness of spirit. We know from our study of 1 Peter that Peter's readers most definitely faced all of the above! And yet to them, dear Peter calmly ends, "Peace to you all who are in Christ Jesus."

And so, as Peter closes his impassioned epistle with this singular word of reminder, "Peace..." how can you and I seek and secure God's peace in our daily life?

Take your tendency to *panic*...and instead
rest in God's *presence.*
Take your tendency to *terror*...and instead
trust in God's wisdom and ways.
Take your tendency to *dread*...and instead
accept God's *dealings.*
Take your tendency to *nervousness*...and instead
know that God is in control.

Peter had been present when the Savior said, "Peace I leave with you, My peace I give to you; not as the world gives do I give to you. Let not your heart be troubled, neither let it be afraid" (John 14:27). And now Peter passes on to us the very essence of the personal and final words Jesus had spoken to Peter and the other disciples as they went on to face their suffering, "Peace to you all who are in Christ Jesus. Amen."

*L*esson 25

Putting On a Gentle and Quiet Spirit

Take a few minutes to scan through each chapter of 1 Peter. Note your personal thoughts here regarding these subjects and how each relates to a gentle and quiet spirit.

Chapter 1—Our Salvation

Chapter 2—Our Savior

Chapter 3—Our Suffering

Chapter 4—Our Activity During Suffering

Chapter 5—Our End After Suffering

"Peace to you all who are in Christ Jesus. Amen."

How to Study the Bible —Some Practical Tips

By Jim George, Th.M.

One of the noblest pursuits a child of God can embark upon is to get to know and understand God better. The best way we can accomplish this is to look carefully at the book He has written, the Bible, which communicates who He is and His plan for mankind. There are a number of ways we can study the Bible, but one of the most effective and simple approaches to reading and understanding God's Word involves three simple steps:

Step 1: Observation—*What does the passage say?*

Step 2: Interpretation—*What does the passage mean?*

Step 3: Application—*What am I going to do about what the passage says and means?*

Observation is the first and most important step in the process. As you read the Bible text, you need to *look* carefully at what is said, and how. Look for:

- *Terms, not words.* Words can have many meanings, but terms are words used in a specific way in a specific context. (For instance, the word *trunk* could apply to a tree, a car, or a storage box. However, when you read, "That tree has a very large trunk," you know exactly what the word means, which makes it a term.)

- *Structure.* If you look at your Bible, you will see that the text has units called *paragraphs* (indented or marked ¶). A paragraph is a complete unit of thought. You can discover the content of the author's message by noting and understanding each paragraph unit.

- *Emphasis.* The amount of space or the number of chapters or verses devoted to a specific topic will reveal the importance of that topic (for example, note the emphasis of Romans 9–11 and Psalm 119).

- *Repetition.* This is another way an author demonstrates that something is important. One reading of 1 Corinthians 13, where the author uses the word "love" nine times in only 13 verses, communicates to us that love is the focal point of these 13 verses.

- *Relationships between ideas.* Pay close attention, for example, to certain relationships that appear in the text:

  —Cause-and-effect: "Well done, good and faithful servant; you were faithful over a few things, I will make you ruler over many things" (Matthew 25:21).
  —Ifs and thens: "If My people who are called by My name will humble themselves, and pray and seek My face, and turn from their wicked ways, then I will hear from heaven and forgive their sin and heal their land" (2 Chronicles 7:14).
  —Questions and answers: "Who is the King of glory? The Lord strong and mighty" (Psalm 24:8).

- *Comparisons and contrasts.* For example, "You have heard that it was said...but I say to you..." (Matthew 5:21).

- *Literary form.* The Bible is literature, and the three main types of literature in the Bible are discourse (the epistles), prose (Old Testament history), and poetry (the Psalms). Considering the type of literature makes a great deal of difference when you read and interpret the Scriptures.

- *Atmosphere.* The author had a particular reason or burden for writing each passage, chapter, and book. Be sure you notice the mood or tone or urgency of the writing.

After you have considered these things, you then are ready to ask the "Wh" questions:

Who?   Who are the people in this passage?
What?   What is happening in this passage?
Where?   Where is this story taking place?
When?   What time (of day, of the year, in history) is it?

Asking these four "Wh" questions can help you notice terms and identify atmosphere. The answers will also enable you to use your imagination to recreate the scene you're reading about.

As you answer the "Wh" questions and imagine the event, you'll probably come up with some questions of your own. Asking those additional questions for understanding will help to build a bridge between observation (the first step) and interpretation (the second step) of the Bible study process.

Interpretation is discovering the meaning of a passage, the author's main thought or idea. Answering the questions that arise during observation will help you in the process of interpretation. Five clues (called "the five C's") can help you determine the author's main point(s):

Context. You can answer 75 percent of your questions about a passage when you read the text. Reading the text involves looking at the near context (the verse immediately before and after) as well as the far context (the paragraph or the chapter that precedes and/or follows the passage you're studying).

Cross-references. Let Scripture interpret Scripture. That is, let other passages in the Bible shed light on the passage you are looking at. At the same time, be careful not to assume that the same word or phrase in two different passages means the same thing.

Culture. The Bible was written long ago, so when we interpret it, we need to understand it from the writers' cultural context.

Conclusion. Having answered your questions for understanding by means of context, cross-reference, and culture, you can make a preliminary statement of the passage's meaning. Remember that if your passage consists of more than one paragraph, the author may be presenting more than one thought or idea.

Consultation. Reading books known as commentaries, which are written by Bible scholars, can help you interpret Scripture.

Application is why we study the Bible. We want our lives to change; we want to be obedient to God and to grow more like Jesus Christ. After we have observed a passage and interpreted or understood it to the best of our ability, we must then apply its truth to our own life.

You'll want to ask the following questions of every passage of Scripture you study:

- How does the truth revealed here affect my relationship with God?
- How does this truth affect my relationship with others?
- How does this truth affect me?
- How does this truth affect my response to the enemy Satan?

The application step is not completed by simply answering these questions; the key is *putting into practice* what God has taught you in your study. Although at any given moment you cannot be consciously applying *every*thing you're learning in Bible study, you can be consciously applying *some*thing. And when you work on applying a truth to your life, God will bless your efforts by, as noted earlier, conforming you to the image of Jesus Christ.

Helpful Bible Study Resources:

Concordance—Young's or Strong's

Bible dictionary—Unger's or Holman's

Webster's dictionary

The Zondervan Pictorial Encyclopedia of the Bible

Manners and Customs of the Bible,
 James M. Freeman

Books on Bible Study:

The Joy of Discovery, Oletta Wald

Enjoy Your Bible, Irving L. Jensen

How to Read the Bible for All It's Worth, Gordon
Fee & Douglas Stuart

A Layman's Guide to Interpreting the Bible,
 W. Henrichsen

Living by the Book, Howard G. Hendricks

*L*eading a Bible Study
Discussion Group

*W*hat a privilege it is to lead a Bible study! And what joy and excitement await you as you delve into the Word of God and help others to discover its life-changing truths. If God has called you to lead a Bible study group, I know you'll be spending much time in prayer and planning and giving much thought to being an effective leader. I also know that taking the time to read through the following tips will help you to navigate the challenges of leading a Bible study discussion group and enjoying the effort and opportunity.

The Leader's Roles

As a Bible study group leader, you'll find your role changing back and forth from *expert* to *cheerleader* to *lover* to *referee* during the course of a session.

Since you're the leader, group members will look to you to be the *expert* guiding them through the material. So be well prepared. In fact, be over-prepared so that you know the material better than any group member does. Start your study early in the week and let its message simmer all week long. (You might even work several lessons ahead so that you have in mind the big picture and the overall direction of the study.) Be ready to share some additional gems that your group members wouldn't have discovered on their own. That extra insight from your study time—or that comment from a wise Bible teacher or scholar, that clever saying, that keen observation from another believer, and even an appropriate joke—adds an element of fun and keeps Bible study from becoming routine, monotonous, and dry.

Second, be ready to be the group's *cheerleader.* Your energy and enthusiasm for the task at hand can be contagious. It can also stimulate people to get more involved in their personal study as well as in the group discussion.

Third, be the *lover,* the one who shows a genuine concern for the members of the group. You're the one who will establish the atmosphere of the group. If you laugh and have fun, the group members will laugh and have fun. If you hug, they will hug. If you care, they will care. If you share, they will share. If you love, they will love. So pray every day to love the women God has placed in your group. Ask Him to show you how to love them with His love.

Finally, as the leader, you'll need to be the *referee* on occasion. That means making sure everyone has an equal opportunity to speak. That's easier to do when you operate under the assumption that every member of the group has something worthwhile to contribute. So, trusting that the Lord has taught each person during the week, act on that assumption.

Expert, cheerleader, lover, and referee—these four roles of the leader may make the task seem overwhelming. But that's not bad if it keeps you on your knees praying for your group.

A Good Start

Beginning on time, greeting people warmly, and opening in prayer gets the study off to a good start. Know what you want to have happen during your time together and make sure those things get done. That kind of order means comfort for those involved.

Establish a format and let the group members know what that format is. People appreciate being in a Bible study that focuses on the Bible. So keep the discussion on the topic and move the group through the questions. Tangents are often hard to avoid—and even harder to rein in. So be sure to focus on the answers to questions about the specific passage at hand. After all, the purpose of the group is Bible study!

Finally, as someone has accurately observed, "Personal growth is one of the by-products of any effective small group. This growth is achieved when people are recognized and accepted by others. The more friendliness, mutual trust, respect, and warmth exhibited, the more likely that the member will find pleasure in the group, and, too, the more likely she will work hard toward the accomplishment of the group's goals. The effective leader will strive to reinforce desirable traits" (source unknown).

A Dozen Helpful Tips

Here is a list of helpful suggestions for leading a Bible study discussion group:

1. Arrive early, ready to focus fully on others and give of yourself. If you have to do any last-minute preparation, review, re-grouping, or praying, do it in the car. Don't dash in, breathless, harried, late, still tweaking your plans.

2. Check out your meeting place in advance. Do you have everything you need—tables, enough chairs, a blackboard, hymnals if you plan to sing, coffee, etc.?

3. Greet each person warmly by name as she arrives. After all, you've been praying for these women all week long, so let each VIP know that you're glad she's arrived.

4. Use name tags for at least the first two or three weeks.

5. Start on time no matter what—even if only one person is there!

6. Develop a pleasant but firm opening statement. You might say, "This lesson was great! Let's get started so we can enjoy all of it!" or "Let's pray before we begin our lesson."

7. Read the questions, but don't hesitate to reword them on occasion. Rather than reading an entire paragraph of instructions, for instance, you might say, "Question 1 asks us to list some ways that Christ displayed humility. Lisa, please share one way Christ displayed humility."

8. Summarize or paraphrase the answers given. Doing so will keep the discussion focused on the topic; eliminate digressions; help avoid or clear up any misunderstandings of the text; and keep each group member aware of what the others are saying.

9. Keep moving and don't add any of your own questions to the discussion time. It's important to get through the study guide questions. So if a cut-and-dried answer is called for, you don't need to comment with anything other than a "thank you." But when the question asks for an opinion or an application (for instance, "How can this truth help us in our marriages?" or "How do *you* find time for your quiet time?"), let all who want to contribute.

10. Affirm each person who contributes, especially if the contribution was very personal, painful to share, or a quiet person's rare statement. Make everyone who shares a hero by saying something like "Thank you for sharing that insight from your own life" or "We certainly appreciate what God has taught you. Thank you for letting us in on it."

11. Watch your watch, put a clock right in front of you, or consider using a timer. Pace the discussion so that you meet your cut-off time, especially if you want time to pray. Stop at the designated time even if you haven't finished the lesson. Remember that everyone has worked through the study once; you are simply going over it again.

12. End on time. You can only make friends with your group members by ending on time or even a little early! Besides,

members of your group have the next item on their agenda to attend to—picking up children from the nursery, babysitter, or school; heading home to tend to matters there; running errands; getting to bed; or spending some time with their husbands. So let them out *on time!*

Five Common Problems

In any group, you can anticipate certain problems. Here are some common ones that can arise, along with helpful solutions:

1. *The incomplete lesson*—Right from the start, establish the policy that if someone has not done the lesson, it is best for her not to answer the questions. But do try to include her responses to questions that ask for opinions or experiences. Everyone can share some thoughts in reply to a question like, "Reflect on what you know about both athletic and spiritual training and then share what you consider to be the essential elements of training oneself in godliness."

2. *The gossip*—The Bible clearly states that gossiping is wrong, so you don't want to allow it in your group. Set a high and strict standard by saying, "I am not comfortable with this conversation," or "We [not *you*] are gossiping, ladies. Let's move on."

3. *The talkative member*—Here are three scenarios and some possible solutions for each.

   a. The problem talker may be talking because she has done her homework and is excited about something she has to share. She may also know more about the subject than the others and, if you cut her off, the rest of the group may suffer.

Solution: Respond with a comment like: "Sarah, you are making very valuable contributions. Let's see if we can get some reactions from the others," or "I know Sarah can answer this. She's really done her homework. How about some of the rest of you?"

b. The talkative member may be talking because she has *not* done her homework and wants to contribute, but she has no boundaries.

Solution: Establish at the first meeting that those who have not done the lesson do not contribute except on opinion or application questions. You may need to repeat this guideline at the beginning of each session.

c. The talkative member may want to be heard whether or not she has anything worthwhile to contribute.

Solution: After subtle reminders, be more direct, saying, "Betty, I know you would like to share your ideas, but let's give others a chance. I'll call on you later."

4. *The quiet member*—Here are two scenarios and possible solutions.

a. The quiet member wants the floor but somehow can't get the chance to share.

Solution: Clear the path for the quiet member by first watching for clues that she wants to speak (moving to the edge of her seat, looking as if she wants to speak, perhaps even starting to say something) and then saying, "Just a second. I think Chris wants to say something." Then, of course, make her a hero!

b. The quiet member simply doesn't want the floor.

Solution: "Chris, what answer do you have on question 2?" or "Chris, what do you think about…?" Usually after a shy person has contributed a few times, she will become more confident and more ready to share. Your role is to provide an opportunity where there is *no* risk of a wrong answer. But occasionally a group member will tell you that she would rather not be called on. Honor her request, but from time to time ask her privately if she feels ready to contribute to the group discussions.

In fact, give all your group members the right to pass. During your first meeting, explain that any time a group member does not care to share an answer, she may simply say, "I pass." You'll want to repeat this policy at the beginning of every group session.

5. *The wrong answer*—Never tell a group member that she has given a wrong answer, but at the same time never let a wrong answer go by.

SOLUTION: Either ask if someone else has a different answer or ask additional questions that will cause the right answer to emerge. As the women get closer to the right answer, say, "We're getting warmer! Keep thinking! We're almost there!"

Learning from Experience

Immediately after each Bible study session, evaluate the group discussion time using this checklist. You may also want a member of your group (or an assistant or trainee or outside observer) to evaluate you periodically.

Notes

1. Elizabeth George, *A Woman After God's Own Heart*™ (Eugene, OR: Harvest House Publishers, 1997), pp. 24-29.

2. W. E. Vine, *An Expository Dictionary of New Testament Words* (Old Tappan, NJ: Fleming H. Revell Company, 1966), pp. 56,242.

3. Robert Jamieson, A. R. Fausset, and David Brown, *Commentary on the Whole Bible* (Grand Rapids, MI: Zondervan Publishing House, 1973), p. 1475.

4. D. L. Moody, *Notes from My Bible and Thoughts from My Library* (Grand Rapids, MI: Baker Book House, 1979), p. 360.

5. A. Naismith, *A Treasury of Notes, Quotes, & Anecdotes* (Grand Rapids, MI: Baker Book House, 1976), p. 211.

6. Matthew Henry, *Commentary on the Whole Bible*—Vol. 6 (Peabody, MA: Hendrickson Publishers, 1996), p. 812.

7. H. D. M. Spence and Joseph S. Exell, *The Pulpit Commentary*—Vol. 22 (Grand Rapids, MI: William B. Eerdmans Publishing Company, 1978), p. 18.

8. Charles F. Pfeiffer and Everett F. Harrison, *The Wycliffe Bible Commentary* (Chicago: Moody Press, 1973), p. 1946.

9. Donald Grey Barnhouse, *Let Me Illustrate* (Grand Rapids, MI: Fleming H. Revell, 1994), pp. 161-62.

10. Eleanor L. Dean, *The Speaker's Sourcebook* (Grand Rapids, MI: Zondervan Publishing House, 1977), p. 154.

11. George, *A Woman After God's Own Heart*™, p. 240.

12. Charles R. Swindoll, *Hope in Hurtful Times* (Fullerton, CA: Insight for Living, 1990), p. 48.

13. *Life Application Bible Commentary—1 Peter, 2 Peter, Jude* (Wheaton, IL: Tyndale House Publishers, Inc., 1995), p. 72.

14. Mrs. Charles E. Cowman, *Streams in the Desert,* Vol. 1 (Grand Rapids, MI: Zondervan Publishing House, 1965), p. 97.

15. Swindoll, *Hope in Hurtful Times,* p. 56.

16. Ibid.

17. John MacArthur, *The MacArthur Study Bible* (Nashville, TN: Word Publishing, 1997), p. 1944.

18. Benjamin R. DeJong, ed., *Uncle Ben's Quotebook* (Grand Rapids, MI: Baker Book House, 1977), p. 246.

19. *Life Application Bible* (Wheaton, IL: Tyndale House Publishers, Inc., 1995), p. 1934.

20. Richard W. DeHaan and Henry G. Bosch, eds., *Our Daily Bread Favorites* (Grand Rapids, MI: Zondervan Publishing House, 1971), April 16.

21. Harry Verploegh, *Oswald Chambers—The Best from All His Books* (Nashville, TN: Oliver-Nelson Books, 1987), pp. 116-17.

22. Richard Halverson, source unknown.

23. M. R. DeHaan and H. G. Bosch, eds., *Bread for Each Day* (Grand Rapids, MI: Zondervan Publishing House, 1980), May 26.

24. Swindoll, *Hope in Hurtful Times*, p. 82

25. *Life Application Bible Commentary*, p. 113.

26. Lyrics and music by John W. Peterson, 1957.

27. Swindoll, *Hope in Hurtful Times,* p. 102, quoting C. S. Lewis, *The Problem of Pain* (New York City: Macmillan Co., 1962), p. 106.

28. *World-Shapers—A Treasury of Quotes from Great Missionaries* (Wheaton, IL: Harold Shaw Publishers, 1991), p. 41.

29. John MacArthur, "Fundamental Attitudes for Spiritual Maturity" (taped 2/25/90, 1 Peter 5:5-14).

30. "Onward, Christian Soldiers" by Sabine Baring-Gould and Arthur S. Sullivan.

31. E. H. Chapin, source unknown.

32. *World-Shapers*, p. 118.

33. Ray Beeson and Ranelda Mack Hunsicker, *The Hidden Price of Greatness* (Wheaton, IL: Tyndale House Publishers, Inc., 1991).

34. J. K. Gressett from *Inspiring Quotations—Contemporary & Classical*, compiled by Albert M. Wells, Jr. (Nashville, TN: Thomas Nelson Publishers, 1988), p. 192.

35. William Barclay, *The Letters of James and Peter* (Philadelphia: The Westminster Press, 1976), p. 273.

36. Ibid., p. 274.

37. Ibid.

38. DeHaan and Bosch, *Bread for Each Day*, January 17.

39. Ibid.

40. Elizabeth George, *A Woman's Walk with God—Growing in the Fruit of the Spirit* (Eugene, OR: Harvest House Publishers, 2000).

Bibliography

Barbieri, Louis A. *1 and 2 Peter—Growing in Grace*. Chicago: Moody Bible Institute of Chicago, 1975.

Barclay, William. *The Letters of James and Peter*. Revised edition. Philadelphia: The Westminster Press, 1976.

Henry, Matthew. *Commentary on the Whole Bible*, Vol. 6. Peabody, MA: Hendrickson Publishers, 1996.

Jensen, Irving L. *1 and 2 Peter*. Chicago: Moody Bible Institute of Chicago, 1971.

Life Application Bible Commentary—1 Peter, 2 Peter, Jude. Wheaton, IL: Tyndale House Publishers, Inc., 1995.

MacArthur, John. *The MacArthur Study Bible*. Nashville, TN: Word Publishing, 1997.

Pfeiffer, Charles F., and Everett F. Harrison. *The Wycliffe Bible Commentary*. Chicago: Moody Press, 1973.

Spence, H. D. M., and Joseph S. Exell. *The Pulpit Commentary*, Vol. 22. Grand Rapids, MI: William B. Eerdmans Publishing Company, 1978.

Swindoll, Charles R. *Hope in Hurtful Times*. Fullerton, CA: Insight for Living, 1990.

Thomas, W. H. Griffith. *The Apostle Peter*. Grand Rapids, MI: Kregel Publications, 1984.

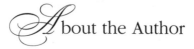bout the Author

Elizabeth George is a bestselling author and speaker whose passion is to teach the Bible in a way that changes women's lives. For information about Elizabeth's books or speaking ministry, to sign up for her mailings, or to share how God has used this book in your life, please write to Elizabeth at:

Elizabeth George
P.O. Box 2879
Belfair, WA 98528

Toll free phone/fax: 1-800-542-4611
www.elizabethgeorge.com

Books by Elizabeth George

Beautiful in God's Eyes—The Treasures of the Proverbs 31 Woman
God Lights My Path—Meditations
The Lord Is My Shepherd—12 Promises for Every Woman
Loving God with All Your Mind
A Woman After God's Own Heart™
A Woman After God's Own Heart™ Audiobook
A Woman After God's Own Heart™ Growth & Study Guide
A Woman After God's Own Heart™ Prayer Journal
A Woman's High Calling—The 10 Essentials of Godly Living
A Woman's High Calling Growth & Study Guide
Women Who Loved God—365 Days with the Women of the Bible
A Woman's Walk with God—Growing in the Fruit of the Spirit
A Woman's Walk with God Growth & Study Guide

A Woman After God's Own Heart™ Bible Study Series

Walking in God's Promises—The Life of Sarah
Becoming a Woman of Beauty & Strength—Esther
Experiencing God's Peace—Philippians
Pursuing Godliness—1 Timothy
Growing in Wisdom & Faith—James
Putting On a Gentle & Quiet Spirit—1 Peter

Children's Books

God's Wisdom for Little Girls—Virtues & Fun from Proverbs 31